Democracy and the state

CAMBRIDGE PERSPECTIVES IN HISTORY
Series editors: Richard Brown and David Smith

Other theme texts in the series include:

Democracy and the state, 1830–1945

Michael Willis

Brentwood School

PUBLISHED BY THE PRESS SYNDICATE OF THE UNIVERSITY OF CAMBRIDGE
The Pitt Building, Trumpington Street, Cambridge CB2 1RP, United Kingdom

CAMBRIDGE UNIVERSITY PRESS
The Edinburgh Building, Cambridge CB2 2RU, United Kingdom
40 West 20th Street, New York, NY 10011–4211, USA
10 Stamford Road, Oakleigh, Melbourne 3166, Australia

First published 1999

Printed in the United Kingdom at the University Press, Cambridge

Typeset in Tiepolo and Formata

A catalogue record for this book is available from the British Library

ISBN 0 521 59994 6 paperback

Text design by Newton Harris Design Partnership

Acknowledgements
Cover, Bridgeman Art Library / Harris Museum and Art Gallery, Preston; 14, 15, 107, Hulton Getty Collection; 36, 37, Mary Evans Picture Library; 45, *Punch*.

The cover illustration by Vladimir Ossipovitch Sherwood depicts a scene from the Preston by-election of 1862.

Contents

Contents

Introduction

In 1830 only about one in ten of adult men in the United Kingdom could vote, whereas almost all men and women could do so by 1945. The House of Commons of 1830 contained no MPs who could be described as working class, whereas in 1945 a mass electorate chose a Labour government drawn from the party which grew up to represent working men and was largely financed by trade unions.

How people were governed is connected with how they lived and thought. Large-scale industry was not yet general in 1830s Britain. Nearly 30 per cent of the workforce was employed in agriculture, and goods like shoes, furniture and carriages were still normally made by local craftsmen. Rule by landowning gentlemen was normal over most of the country. British workers did get ideas about people power from the French Revolution. Campaigners and writers like Sir Francis Burdett and Jeremy Bentham supported democracy in the 1810s and 1820s, but the politicians in parliament and local government overwhelmingly opposed it. We normally call something democratic when we approve of it; 1830s politicians, unlike us, condemned and feared democracy. Early nineteenth-century electors did not generally think in democratic terms, and Chapter 1 explains how their ideas about voting differed from today's.

People saw the state differently as well. It existed mainly to defend the country and keep law and order. Workers had ideas about how the government should safeguard their wages and working conditions in line with traditions from Tudor times, but people in power did not accept this. Low-paid handloom weavers appealed to the government to improve their conditions. The Royal Commission on Handloom Weavers in 1840 told them that they should 'flee from the trade' as no ruler could raise their wages, and this was the general view of England's governors. Many poorer people thought they had a right to poor relief – help from the local taxes known as poor rates – but the government and ratepayers were increasingly reluctant to provide this. Few people thought the government had a duty to provide education, housing or health care or to help find work for the unemployed. Ideas had changed hugely by 1945.

Chapters 1–3 explain how parliamentary elections and the House of Commons became more democratic between 1830 and 1945. Chapter 4 indicates how power shifted between different parts of the government and helps show how much control electors and their MPs actually gained. Chapters 5–7 outline how ideas about the state's responsibilities changed and how its role altered and increased. The conclusion assesses how far Britain has become a democracy and how much attitudes to the state have altered since 1945.

1 The Great Reform Act and the reformed electoral system, 1830–1867

Before 1832 the electoral system was unrepresentative in many obvious ways, although recent historians have found evidence of the power of the people in some boroughs. The 1832 Reform Act gave the vote to more people and distributed MPs more reasonably, but it had mixed effects. It was a result of both politicians' manoeuvres and popular pressure; historians disagree about the relative importance of these. The Whig government which introduced the act was strongly opposed to democracy. Between 1832 and 1867 political parties developed spasmodically, and often concentrated most on local elections.

Voting in the nineteenth century

Modern general elections are about which party will form the next government. Television coverage is crucial, and commentators puzzle over the impact of popular newspapers. Nationally, the parties spend as much money as they can beg or borrow and devote themselves to advertising and the art of spin doctoring – attempting to persuade or trick the media into presenting news in the way most favourable for their own side. Locally, candidates in individual *constituencies** (the areas which elect MPs) are strictly limited in their campaign spending and expect electors to decide mainly according to national issues.

In the early nineteenth century elections were fought far more on local issues. Election spending was unlimited. Increasing numbers of candidates used the national party labels of Whig and Tory but, whereas we weigh up images of competing party leaders seen on television, the elector of 1830 would be more likely to consider loyalty to local landed families and community rivalries. A growing national press informed people of how the government was governing and misspending their money. Satirists ridiculed politicians, and cartoonists showed their uglier physical features, but without film their faces and voices remained largely unknown to most voters. Their speeches could be read in great detail in the quality newspapers bought by a wealthy elite, but there was not much of a national campaign.

Research based on *opinion polls* shows that modern voters are strongly influenced by personal economic expectations – how far they think they and their families are becoming better off under the current government – and that they base their choice of whom to support on national indicators like interest

---

* Words that are explained in the glossary on pages 117–18 appear in *italics*.

rates and taxation. Although opinion polling has only developed in Britain since the 1930s, there is plenty of evidence that early nineteenth-century men also voted according to what was economically best for themselves and their families. There was much propaganda against taxes which hit the poor, but voters' key economic questions were often local and personal. What financial advantages or new facilities did candidates offer their town? What might they gain in the way of *patronage* – jobs for themselves or their families? How much free food and drink were available during the election campaign, and how much cash could they gain from their support? In addition, voting was public; a man might have to follow his employer's or landlord's wishes to keep his job or his house.

This does not mean that the electors were merely selling their votes or cowering before threats. Sometimes, no doubt, they were, but a nineteenth-century man frequently expected to follow the lead of his social superiors, and such 'deference' was strongest in rural areas and small communities. Free food, drink and cash were often seen as an appropriate return from the candidate a voter wanted to support anyway. The key difference between the voting mentality then and now is that, for us, the vote is a democratic right, whereas for nineteenth-century electors it was more a property to be made use of and so an extra source of income. The old system of representation involved not just different election rules, but a different way of thinking. Rules could be altered by law in a single year, but thinking changed slowly over generations.

The old system of representation

The old system of electing MPs was based on laws and traditions which often dated back to medieval times. It developed piecemeal over centuries rather than logically. It was not representative in a way that modern political thinkers would accept – MPs were neither typical of the population nor elected by any method that made statistical sense. Moreover, in some ways the system was becoming more unrepresentative. Industrial towns like Manchester and Birmingham, which were developing into some of the largest cities in England, sent no representatives to parliament, though any substantial property owners there could help choose MPs for their counties. Yet an uninhabited mound in southern England called Old Sarum – site of the medieval forerunner of Salisbury – chose two MPs, or to be more precise its owner chose them.

The number of voters grew, but not as fast as the population. Since there was no permanent register of electors we shall never know what proportion of adults could vote, but one carefully compiled estimate suggests it fell from almost 20 per cent of adult men in 1715 to around 12 per cent in 1831. In Scotland it was well under 1 per cent in the early 1800s and in Ireland the numbers were reduced by a new property qualification in 1829 to about 2–3 per cent.

The majority of MPs were elected from *boroughs* – towns or small settlements which had gained the right over centuries from medieval times – and only 16 per cent of England's MPs came from the other county areas, where over half the electors voted. The arrangements for voting in boroughs were again a matter of tradition, the number of electors varying from a handful to over 10,000. Almost half the MPs were nominated by so-called patrons – wealthy men who could control borough elections and were said to have the borough in their 'pocket'. J. W. Croker, a particularly well-informed electoral manipulator, estimated 276 out of 658 MPs were chosen by such 'patrons'.[1]

Can the old system be justified?

When a system is described like this, it is hard to understand how anybody who did not have a selfish interest in it could defend it. Yet many did, and late twentieth-century historians have been busy finding out that it had considerable merits. As often happens in history, the problem is working out what is typical and what is unusual. Some small borough electorates may have voted according to their landlords' orders in a grovelling manner, but historians like O'Gorman, Phillips and Vernon[2] have discovered a lively kind of people's politics in many of the larger boroughs. Records show that a majority of those voting in many borough elections were working people. Over 80 per cent of the electors in boroughs like Boston and Lewes were shopkeepers, craftsmen or unskilled labourers.

Our politics is a rather private affair; informed by television and newspapers we vote secretly in a polling booth. Their politics was riotous street theatre with bands and processions; candidates shouted their speeches, audiences heckled and electors voted on a public platform. O'Gorman emphasises how patrons and politicians carried on a dialogue with the voters, whose support could not be taken for granted. Sometimes an election crowd furthered the interchange with roof tiles and rotting vegetables, but often there was more intelligent bargaining and consultation. The public election rituals certainly allowed the people – both electors and non-electors – to tell the candidates what they thought of them.

The old system was not intended, like ours, to represent the people numerically; it was to represent property and economic interests. Hence it was property owners who voted, and wealthy men with money from land, trade or industry bought influence over others. The striking anomalies in the system brought strong demands for reform in the 1780s, especially among wealthy country gentry, but in the 1790s the French Revolution showed that moderate reform schemes could end in bloody chaos. The English system might not be rational, but at least it was stable. Why then did change come in 1832 after decades during which reformers had despaired of success?

Why did reform come in 1832?

Differing explanations

There are two sides to any explanation of parliamentary reform – how strongly the public were campaigning for it, and what politicians were doing among themselves. Any convincing overall explanation involves both, but the relative importance of the two has kept historians arguing for decades. Many historians emphasise pressure from campaigners and an exploited *working class* in gaining reform from reluctant politicians, and this view which stresses people power is attractive to left-wing historians. Others – often labelled the 'high politics' school – while not necessarily denying that public agitation has influence, emphasise that reform measures can be wholly or mainly accounted for by manoeuvres among politicians to gain and retain power. This explanation, which stresses the role of the political elite rather than the people, is often more attractive to right wingers.

Added to this are questions about what motivated public and politicians. How far can popular agitation be explained by hunger and distress? How far was it the result of growing political consciousness among the working class, which committed left-wing historians often stress? How far are politicians motivated by political principles which 'high politics' historians tend to play down?

Pressure from the people

Working-class pressure for parliamentary reform grew markedly after 1815, increasing in times of hardship like 1816–19, when reform clubs proliferated and labouring families attended gigantic reform meetings. While pressure declined with greater prosperity in the mid-1820s, it had intensified again by 1830 when the poor harvest of 1829 increased food prices and unemployment apparently rose; reform petitions then gained unprecedented numbers of signatures.

By this time *middle-class* industrialists, traders and financiers who believed strongly in the need for industrial towns to be represented in parliament were providing support and leadership for the movement – some, like Thomas Attwood from Birmingham, taking the initiative in forming political unions of employers and workers. Pressure for reform became most intense once a Whig government had introduced a parliamentary reform bill (a proposal for a law), but it had built up previously and was not just a response to initiatives from leading politicians.

It is hard to estimate the role of radical thought – ideas about changing government fundamentally from its roots. To a great extent, *radicalism* came from the French Revolution, which probably deterred, more than it encouraged, support for change. Whilst the radical book by Tom Paine, *Rights of man*, published in 1791–92, had been popular and influential, far more people had read the anti-reforming pamphlets of writers like Hannah More in the 1790s.

After 1815 radical newspapers like William Cobbett's *Political Register* were very widely read, and they expanded in numbers and circulation in the late 1820s. Ideas of fundamental reform obviously seemed most necessary and attractive when hardship was greatest, and there was a variety of ideas from which to choose. Some radicals based their arguments on the Rights of Man, as did Paine and the French revolutionaries; others on how they thought England had been governed in the past. Some demanded the vote for all adult men; others claimed it only for householders.

Whilst there was little agreed theory, an extraordinarily wide range of men came to support parliamentary reform because they hoped for different things from it. Some saw it as a beginning for a new type of politics in which the middle class would gain power or as a start on the road to democracy. Others hoped it would restore an older, more honest type of politics by reducing the government's ability to control elections through bribes and threats and thought that a more popularly elected House of Commons would make ministers less corrupt and dictatorial. Radicals wanted a differently elected parliament to speed up change, whereas a few extreme Tories supported electoral reform in order to slow it down.

Politicians' beliefs and calculations

The 'high politics' explanation for the 1832 Reform Act starts with the disintegration of the Tory leadership who supported the old system in the late 1820s. There was a strong religious side to Tory politics. The Tory party existed to maintain the privileges of the Church of England and its moderate type of Protestant religion, just as the party stood for the old way of government; indeed the two were closely interconnected, with a law banning Roman Catholics from being MPs and holding various government offices. Yet in 1829, under irresistible pressure from Ireland – where a large majority of the population was Roman Catholic – the Duke of Wellington's Tory government removed the ban, granting what was known as Catholic Emancipation. More extreme Tories – so-called ultras – saw this as betrayal. For the ultras Catholic Emancipation itself was the beginning of a dangerous revolution. There were many signs that popular opinion in the country was against it and hence many ultras came to think that giving more people the vote might be the best way of maintaining the parts of England's constitution which really mattered, even if at first sight parliamentary reform seemed to alter or undermine it. Lord Winchilsea announced that whatever doubts he previously had about reform had been removed by Tory leaders; the Marquis of Blandford introduced reform bills in 1829 and 1830; the Duke of Richmond was a member of the Whig cabinet which undertook reform; and 28 ultras voted for the First Reform Bill in 1831.

The Tory party, which had provided the main resistance to reform, was crumbling as Wellington upset both moderates and extremists in the party. Lacking adequate support by the end of 1830, he had to resign and was replaced by the Whig leader, Lord Grey, who formed a government from not only the Whigs but also from radicals (left wingers who wanted large-scale change), moderate Tories and ultras. 'High politics' historians explain the First Reform Act largely in terms of Grey's immediate political needs. He needed some key issue to unite a varied cabinet and consolidate a diverse parliamentary following behind the government. Reform was the answer. It would help the Whigs, who had been out of office for over twenty years, to gain a popular following, and it gave them a chance to alter the electoral system to their own advantage. The small boroughs they abolished were generally Tory strongholds, and the £10 householders – those who owned or occupied property that could be let for at least £10 a year – to whom they gave the vote in the towns were largely Whig supporters.

Another explanation is that Grey simply believed in parliamentary reform – a simple interpretation, but a reasonable one. Grey had been a long-standing champion of reform, proposing it in the House of Commons in 1793 and 1797, and his measure in 1831 was similar to the proposals he had put forward earlier when he was the leading parliamentary spokesman for the *aristocratic* reform group Friends of the People. Admittedly, he had abandoned hope of achieving reform in the 1820s, but it is not surprising that he should return to his old policies once principle, opportunity and political advantage pointed in the same direction. People's beliefs often coincide with their self-interest, but that does not mean they are insincere. Historians' explanations, whether expressed in terms of principle or pressure of events or political advantage, often conflict, but they may also be combined and used to complement each other.

Principles behind the reform

Whatever the motives, there has been little controversy about the basic principles of the Whig reform. These were not democratic. Grey was a great landowning nobleman who wanted to preserve aristocratic power and saw that the best way of doing so was by making tactical concessions. As he put it in a private letter,[3] the middle class 'who form the real and efficient mass of public opinion, and without whom the power of the gentry is nothing' demanded reform. Once given a share of power they would help defend the constitution. They were, as one Whig MP explained, 'the natural allies' of law and order who needed to be won over to help resist democracy, and hence the First Reform Act was the 'best security against Revolution'. Whig leaders emphasised that it was to be a final settlement.

As the table on page 9 shows, Scotland and Ireland had separate reform acts from England in 1832. Ireland had a different system of registration and a far smaller county electorate, and much depended on decisions by landowners and registration officers. As a result only 1 in 146 people in Ireland had a vote by 1850 compared with 1 in 19 in England. The Irish Franchise Act of 1850 increased this to 1 person in 40 by altering the registration procedure and introducing a new county voting qualification based on occupying property.

The results of reform

There are different ways of assessing what was achieved. Most modern judgements are based on our own democratic values. We concentrate on how many more people got the vote, though this alone is a very inadequate basis for judging. *How* people voted, how much opportunity they actually had to vote in elections and what choice of candidates they had are crucial. Most important of all is how the constituencies were arranged, for this determines how much power different groups of voters really had.

The increase in the electorate does not seem very impressive when looked at by numbers. It is difficult to calculate how many people could vote because some had several votes, but O'Gorman calculates that in England it rose from 12.7 per cent to 18 per cent of adult men. In Scotland the increase was more dramatic, and the electorate increased from 4,000 to 65,000, though this was still only about

Simplified summary of changes under the 1832 Reform Acts

		Before	After
Who could vote in boroughs?	England and Wales	Varied traditional arrangements	£10 householders (men who owned or occupied property which could be let for at least £10 rent a year) Others who had voted before kept vote for life as long as they lived within 7 miles of borough
	Scotland	Delegates from town councils, but these were controlled by wealthy landowners	£10 householders as in England
	Ireland	Varied traditional arrangements	£10 householders as in England Others who had voted before kept vote for life
Who could vote in counties?	England and Wales	40-shilling freeholders (owners of property which could be let for at least £2 rent a year)	40-shilling freeholders Men with copyhold land (a traditional type of long-term land tenure) worth at least £10 rent a year Men leasing or renting land for at least £50 a year
	Scotland	Those with traditional rights over land worth at least £70–130 a year in rent	£10 freeholders (owners of property which could be let for at least £10 rent a year) Tenants could vote as in England with a few extra restrictions
	Ireland	£10 freeholders (owners of land which could be let for at least £10 rent a year)	£10 freeholders Men leasing land for at least £10 a year with leases for at least 20 years
How were constituencies organised?	England	Each borough and county elected 2 MPs (with a few exceptions)	Boroughs with under 2,000 population generally lost both MPs Those with roughly 2,000–4,000 population kept 1 MP Extra MPs allocated to counties and new boroughs (large towns without their own MPs before)
	Wales	Each county elected 1 MP and boroughs grouped together to elect MPs	Similar system to that before 1832 with 4 extra MPs
	Scotland	Counties generally had 1 MP and boroughs grouped together to elect MPs	Similar system to that before 1832, but boroughs gained 8 more MPs
	Ireland	Each county elected 2 MPs and each borough generally 1 MP	4 extra MPs given to boroughs and 1 extra MP to Dublin University

12 per cent of adult men; in Ireland about 5 per cent of adult men could vote. As voting was still public, many people cannot have felt truly free to vote as they wished, though a greater proportion of electors gained the chance to express their views. There had only been contests in about a third of constituencies before the First Reform Act, and many electors never or rarely got the chance to vote; no one at all voted in Scotland in the 1826 general election or in Wales in the 1830 election. Between the First (1832) and Second (1867) Reform Acts on average there were contests in over half the constituencies, though the number varied considerably from one election to another.

There was an extensive rearrangement of constituencies, but although the worst anomalies were removed, they were nowhere near equal in population. While parliamentary boroughs contained about 43 per cent of the electorate, they chose 62 per cent of the MPs. Boroughs with over 4,000 people had two MPs; Liverpool with over 202,000 inhabitants had two, as did the Essex borough of Maldon with 4,895.

There was a new uniform qualification for voting in boroughs – living in a house worth £10 a year in rent – but some boroughs already had a large number of working-class electors who did not pay as much as this. As long as they lived in or near the borough these electors could continue to vote during their lifetime, but future generations in the same position would not have the same right. The new uniform qualification, which increased the electorate in most boroughs, consequently reduced it in others.

The type of candidates and the sort of people who became MPs changed little. The political diarist Charles Greville commented that the new House of Commons elected after the 1832 act looked 'much like every other parliament'; MPs still had to own large amounts of landed property and, although there were ways round this qualification, poor men could not enter parliament without wealthy backing. MPs were not paid, and election contests required time and money. With public voting, large sums were still spent on corrupting electors, but now they were more widely distributed than before. Historians have generally accepted Norman Gash's[4] calculation that about seventy MPs were effectively chosen by patrons who could control or influence a majority of electors in 'pocket boroughs'. In view of all this, it is not surprising that after the First Reform Act 70–80 per cent of MPs were still identifiably from the landowning class, and this altered little until the 1860s.

Historians' judgement on the First Reform Act is generally that it was most important as a first step. Once the constitution was significantly changed it would be easier to gain further alterations. Although many Tories opposed the act for just this reason, people at the time judged it more by its immediate effects than by its long-term possibilities. How far did it meet middle- and working-class expectations?

Effects for different classes

The new borough electorate was generally middle class; as property values varied so did the proportion of people enfranchised by the £10 householder qualification. One Whig minister accepted that the proportion of houses worth £10 a year varied from about a sixth to a half between different towns. The middle class substantially gained the vote, but that did not necessarily mean power. Electors could be pressured in all kinds of ways – tenants by landowners, professional men by upper-class clients, shopkeepers by working-class customers. The small number of working MPs contrasted with the landed majority; for instance, under 100 out of 658 MPs were bankers, merchants or manufacturers. This was scarcely the political power which some class-conscious businessmen thought they deserved, while large numbers of *Nonconformists* among the middle class saw landed predominance in government maintaining unacceptable privileges for the Church of England.

Working-class disappointment was greater. Vast numbers of working men attended meetings in support of Grey's reform bill, and it is impossible to know how well they knew its details or what they expected from it. In reality the act reduced the number of working-class electors in some boroughs. Henry Hetherington, the editor of the *Poor Man's Guardian*, described the act as 'an invitation to the shopocrats of the enfranchised towns to join the Whigocrats of the country, and make common cause with them in keeping down the people'. The reformed House of Commons did little to improve the workers' position in the 1830s, and the 1834 Poor Law Amendment Act apparently withdrew the traditional right of the poor to help in their own homes in times of hardship. It led to bitter resentment. One Essex weaver refused to do some hard labour required under the poor law, protesting that 'he had been for Reform and this was what they had got by it'. Between 1838 and 1848 massive numbers of working-class people supported the Chartist movement, which campaigned for manhood suffrage (a vote for all adult men), secret voting and equal-sized constituencies – in other words, male democracy.

The Whig leaders' success has to be judged according to their own aims, and they had always intended to resist democracy by getting middle-class support for landed power. The landowners' continued predominance, widespread middle-class acquiescence and the small extent of radical activity in 1848, when revolutions spread across Europe, all show Whig success, but the Whigs expected their new arrangement to be a final one. It lasted for 35 years.

The growth of party politics

Most MPs were identifiable as Whigs or Tories in the 1820s and party labels were normally used at elections, but the First Reform Act created a greater need for party organisation. Electoral registers were drawn up for the first time to record who was qualified to vote, and the property qualifications were so complex that claims were being perpetually challenged in the revising courts set up to deal with disputes over who could vote. Politicians tried to ensure that as many of their supporters and as few of their opponents as possible were registered, and agents were needed to do this year by year, not just at election time. While influential local landowners often organised support in counties and small boroughs, extra administration was often needed to win voters in larger towns which sent MPs to parliament for the first time or had enlarged electorates. Local parties were invaluable for these jobs, and the more important national rather than local issues became, the more necessary some national network to mobilise support seemed.

Consequently both the main parties developed a similar structure. They had a central organisation in London with a political agent or manager, committees and a club for wealthy politicians in the capital – the Carlton Club for Conservatives and the Reform Club for Liberals. The central organisation managed funds and made contact with local agents and associations who would put up candidates, register voters and run campaigns. Associations to get people registered and attract more popular support frequently grew up alongside drinking and dining clubs which wealthy party supporters had formed in earlier years. Being in opposition in the 1830s, the Conservatives felt the greatest need to act and, by 1841, had formed hundreds of local associations, especially in larger towns. The Liberals responded to this. In Liverpool, for instance, the Tradesmen's Conservative Association founded in 1836 was soon followed by the Liberal Tradesmen's Reform Association.

How far most electors voted for a candidate as a party representative rather than as an individual is hard to know. Since most constituencies had two MPs and their electors two votes each, one good indicator is whether electors used both their votes for men of the same party. One extensive survey found that the percentage of electors who split their votes between parties fell from an average of 21.9 per cent in the 1818–31 period to 13.9 per cent in 1832–65.[5] Although these figures suggest the First Reform Act dramatically increased party voting, that is a gross oversimplification. Research has shown how in some boroughs, like Shrewsbury and Northampton, it was the controversy over parliamentary reform as a big national issue in 1830–31 which fostered national party loyalties. In others, like Beverley, stronger party loyalties developed after the 1835 Municipal Corporations Act.

Furthermore, the growth in party feeling was irregular. The names 'Liberal' and 'Conservative' replaced 'Whig' and 'Tory' as normal party labels during the 1830s, and the 1841 election was remarkably partisan. Gladstone commented on how the 'principle of party' had 'long predominated' and now had 'a sway almost unlimited'. Yet from the mid-1840s to late 1850s it weakened as parties split up and only intensified again after the 1857 election. In some boroughs national party organisation developed only in the 1860s, as at Lewes where the Conservative Association was formed in 1865 and the Liberal Registration Society in 1866.

The explanation lies partly in the kind of issues which characterised national politics. Controversial religious issues in the 1830s helped polarise voters; around 90 per cent of Nonconformists were Liberal, and *Anglican* priests were over-whelmingly Conservative. Later, economic and social issues often divided parties; the Conservative split over the corn laws in 1846 weakened their organisation, and Sir Robert Peel's leadership does much to explain changing party loyalties.

Modern politics is strongly based on the mandate theory – that voters who support a party candidate are approving a national manifesto which the party carries out if it gets into government. The 'Tamworth Manifesto' that Peel produced for the 1835 election was issued to electors in Peel's own constituency (the area which returned him as an MP); although it was not a national party manifesto, other Conservative candidates could support it if they wished, so it could form the basis of a national appeal. When Peel was prime minister, however, he thought in traditional terms of serving the monarch in the national interest and making decisions according to what he judged best – on his own 'conception', as he put it. In 1841 Peel and other Conservative candidates told the electorate they supported the corn laws, but in 1845 he decided it was in the national interest to abolish them. The leader of the best-organised party was acting against the principles of modern party politics.

Local elections

Party politics was often centred more around local government than national government. Indeed the greatest advances towards democracy were made in local election regulations. The elections for poor law guardians under the 1834 Poor Law Amendment Act and for town councils under the 1835 Municipal Corporations Act were made by what we would call a postal ballot – voting papers were delivered to electors' homes so that they could vote privately when it suited them. People who paid rates (local taxes) themselves could vote and in most, though not all, boroughs this apparently resulted in a larger electorate for town council elections than parliamentary ones, though poorer householders were excluded and there were not many working-class voters until changes in the way the ratebooks were kept after 1850. Council elections were held on a one ratepayer, one vote basis, but wealthy men might have up to six votes for elections to various boards – like the poor law guardians – depending on the property they had.

Party organisation was developed for both national and local elections, and local council voting was often on national party lines, but there were far more local contests than national ones. There could be seven years between general elections, although in practice they came more frequently. Some borough councillors were elected every year, and there were also periodic elections for a mass of other bodies. Ratepayers might have an opportunity to vote not only for poor law guardians but for vestries which managed local parish affairs; improvement commissioners which provided public services like water, sewerage or lighting; and sometimes, after 1848, for a local board of health. The issues in these elections often seemed more clear cut than the ones in national politics, involving very down-to-earth arguments about costs and benefits. Residents in the Essex town of Halstead divided into the 'Clean' and 'Dirty' parties over a water and sewerage scheme in 1854. As local opinion could be sharply divided, these controversies provided excellent material for local politicians. At Leeds, for example, a local water supply scheme became an issue between Liberals who proposed a public one under their control and Tories who favoured provision by a private company. Electors generally identified with one party which they supported in different types of contest, and an emotive or popular issue could be used at different types of election. The Tories successfully used attacks on the poor law reforms to win both town council and parliamentary elections at Nottingham in 1840–41.

How people participated in politics

There was not just more participation than before in mid-nineteenth-century politics, but a different type of participation. It was male ratepayers who elected local councils and committees and generally ratepayers who voted at parliamentary elections. Others may have felt increasingly excluded from politics. The 1832 Reform Act and the 1835 Municipal Corporations Act stated that only men could vote, specifically excluding women from local and national elections.

There was a gradual reduction in the street theatre aspect of elections. More meetings took place in halls or pubs, with admission by ticket. Local politicians increasingly publicised their views by issuing printed sheets. Handbills were often stuck up around the streets, more campaign leaflets were posted to electors and newspapers became more important, so that by the 1850s there were arrangements for press reporters at most political meetings. More local parties and printed information meant better ordered, perhaps better-informed people's politics, but a politics increasingly organised for literate ratepayers.

The growth of national parties, their influence in local elections and the growing use of newspapers all suggest movement towards more modern politics, but this was more a feature of the large towns than the countryside, and elections were still very rough affairs. Benjamin Disraeli had pieces of pork waved in his face during his early political career because he was Jewish. One Conservative MP was removed from his seat after the 1865 election because he had encouraged a riot against his opponents; Sir Robert Clifton told his supporters they would 'butcher' the Liberals. They duly attacked the Liberal party headquarters, and a mob of 30,000 was reported in the market-place, breaking windows and throwing rotten vegetables. In Ireland there were a number of deaths at election time. The Sligo local paper quite casually listed people killed, maimed and left for dead in disturbances.

Landowners still had great influence, as did large urban employers. National laws and trends were not always reflected in local practice. There were laws against bribery in 1841, 1852 and 1854, and yet many electors still expected money for their votes. Poor weavers at Sudbury were so ready to swear on oath that they did not take bribes when they really did, that the local clergyman feared for their souls. He made an arrangement with the candidates' election agents that voters would not have to take the oath so that, even if they were corrupt, at least they would not tell a damnable lie. Large-scale 'treating' remained normal in Maldon, where pub landlords could 'make almost unlimited charges' and two

J. and C. Dodd. *View of Tonbridge during the late election, 18 December, 1832* (top) and *The nomination at Kennington Park for the Lambeth election in 1865*, published in the *Illustrated London News*. What do these pictures of elections show about popular participation in politics and the atmosphere at elections? How far do they suggest that street politics continued and changed between 1832 and 1865? (Look carefully at the figures at the front of the Lambeth scene.)

candidates ran up bills of about £5,000 in 1847. In 1859 it was reported that about a fifth of the electorate at Berwick would not vote unless paid. Despite a law of 1858 abolishing the property qualifications for MPs, the first working-class men did not enter parliament until 1874. Although politics was becoming more partisan, in the mid-nineteenth century one of a candidate's proudest boasts was still often personal independence. How much had political thinking and methods really changed by the 1860s?

Document case study

The impact of the First Reform Act on different classes

1.1 What some people thought before the act was passed

William Holsworthy quotes 'ridiculous' views he heard about the First Reform Bill

'Farmer so and so who thinks that the Reform Bill will abolish all rent and tithes;' – 'this or that mechanic thinks that henceforth bread will be had for nothing, and that there will be no further necessity for labour;' 'such and such an Irishman thinks it will lead to an equalisation of property', – and such like unfounded and senseless notions, which it is by no means improbable that a few poor ignorant fellows may entertain.

Source: J. A. Phillips, *The Great Reform Bill in the boroughs, English electoral behaviour, 1818–1841*, Oxford, 1992, pp. 21–22

1.2 What some people thought after the act was passed

The Chartist leader Robert Lowery describes widespread disappointment after the bill became law

The Bill was carried, but popular expectations had been formed not easily realised. The working man thought that the enfranchised middle classes did not do what they might to attempt to realise them, but that they looked more to their own class interests than to those of the unenfranchised who had helped them to attain the Bill . . . This produced feelings of disappointment and vexation among the working classes towards the middle classes, and a current of popular distrust and ill-feeling set in strongly against them and the Whigs, whose strength they were thought to compose.

Source: E. A. Smith, *Reform or revolution, a diary of reform in England, 1830–2*, Stroud, 1992, pp. 143–44

1.3 A government minister's view

The Whig minister Lord John Russell explains his intentions in introducing the bill

At the time the Reform Bill passed, I stated my belief that it must necessarily give a preponderance to the landed interest; and although it may be deemed that such a preponderance has been somewhat unduly given, I still think that a preponderance in favour of that interest tends to the stability of the general institutions of the country.

Source: Hansard, 3rd series, vol. 39, quoted in D. G Wright, *Democracy and reform 1815–85*, London, 1970, pp. 120–21

1 (a) Whom did the people described in Document 1.1 believe would benefit from the First Reform Act? (b) Whom does Document 1.2 suggest benefited from it? (c) Whom does Document 1.3 suggest would keep predominant power after it was passed?

2 Why did many men believe the First Reform Act would bring drastic changes when the Whig leaders did not intend them?

3 How far did the middle class look to their own class interests after the First Reform Act, as Document 1.2 suggests?

Notes and references

1 M. Brock, *The Great Reform Act*, London, 1973, p. 34.

2 F. O'Gorman, *Voters, patrons and parties: the unreformed electoral system of Hanoverian England, 1734–1832*, Oxford, 1989; J. A. Phillips, *Electoral behaviour in unreformed England*, Princeton, 1982; J. Vernon, *Politics and the people: a study in English political culture, 1815–67*, Cambridge, 1993.

3 Grey to Palmerston, cited in J. Cannon, *Parliamentary reform, 1640–1832*, 2nd edn, Cambridge, 1980, p. 245.

4 N. Gash, *Politics in the age of Peel*, revised edn, London, 1977, Chapter 9.

5 G. W. Cox, *The efficient secret, the cabinet and the development of political parties in Victorian England*, Cambridge, 1987, p. 105.

The extension of the franchise and its results, 1867–1914

There were big extensions of the vote in 1867 and 1886. The Second Reform Act in 1867 gave the vote to large numbers of town workers, and the Third Reform Act in 1884–85 also gave it to most men in country areas. There is disagreement among historians about whether the 1867 act was due to politicians' manoeuvres or popular pressure, but there was much less agitation or controversy over the 1884–85 measures, which produced the modern pattern of single-member constituencies. There was great growth in local party political activity between the reform acts, and fierce controversy later developed about whether women should have the vote.

Why did reform occur in 1867?

Differing explanations

The Second Reform Act introduced by the Conservative leader Benjamin Disraeli in 1867 drastically altered a political system which some Whigs of the 1830s had hoped would last for ever, and this led in turn to a series of further reforms. Historians have divided sharply over whether to explain the act by people power or politicians' plots and manoeuvres. In the 1960s the left-wing Marxist historian Royden Harrison argued for the force of people power, in particular through the mass meetings which the Reform League held in Hyde Park in defiance of a government ban. The right-wing historian Maurice Cowling countered that the explanation lay in the game plans of political leaders using parliamentary reform as a way to outsmart their rivals, and his complex argument did much to inspire a succession of 'high politics' historians (see p. 6).[1]

Popular interest in parliamentary reform died away after the collapse of the democratic Chartist movement in the late 1840s, though there were signs of revival in the 1860s. The Reform League and the Reform Union, both founded in 1864, demanded change, but the agitation mainly developed after leading politicians took up the issue in 1866, and there was little violence compared to the tumultuous riots of the early nineteenth century. Even so, there were disturbances at Hyde Park in July 1866, crowds of over 100,000 were reported at some northern meetings and the agitation must have awakened memories of earlier unrest.

Several MPs used the disturbances as an argument for agreeing reform before pressure increased. Writing to a cabinet colleague, Disraeli explained one of his most important tactical concessions in parliament, at least in part, by a wish 'to destroy the present agitation'. Yet both Disraeli and the Conservative prime minister, Lord Derby, were considering parliamentary reform proposals before the Hyde Park riots or the major northern meetings, and most historians now explain the key developments over reform in terms of party politics at Westminster. How far then were the proposals dictated by the politicians' beliefs or by their tactics to gain and retain power?

Gladstone's bill

A Liberal government started the first bill for reform in 1866–67. Gladstone, who introduced it as leader of the House of Commons, had stated back in 1864 that 'every man' who was not ruled out by 'some consideration of personal unfitness or of political danger' was entitled to a vote. He made this declaration on the day that a delegation of working men came to ask if trade unions could invest in the Post Office Savings Bank. To what extent was Gladstone impressed by the responsibility of working men who now managed large sums of money in co-operative societies, friendly societies and trade unions? Was he expecting that reform would come and taking care to present himself as the working man's friend? When he introduced his bill in 1866, Gladstone ran through the arithmetic, showing how his proposals would give the vote to skilled and industrious workmen but not to many 'mere hand labourers'. It all suggested careful calculation and clear principles, but the successful bill came from Disraeli, who apparently started with clear principles but seemed happy to abandon them as he steered his legislation through the Commons.

Disraeli's proposals and why they were altered

Before the Second Reform Act Disraeli had proposed a reform bill in 1859 extending the vote to limited groups of people, including some skilled workmen whom he praised for their virtue and intelligence; after the act he presented it as a deliberate move to restore political power to working men who had lost voting rights in 1832. He also suggested that Conservatives were ready to trust ordinary people to think and act in the national interest, whereas Liberals saw society as more divided and selfish. He claimed that workers were as 'interested' as any other class in 'the stability and even in the glory' of Britain. He also had some grounds for believing that the Conservatives would benefit electorally from a more generous extension of the vote; the poll books which recorded people's votes before the secret ballot show that labourers were more likely than craftsmen or shopkeepers to be Tories.

Disraeli's justifications were reasonable, but he altered his line in the Commons according to parliamentary circumstances; his actions seemed tactical rather than principled. He accepted or rejected amendments more according to who introduced them than to what they specified. A month after opposing a suggestion from his rival Gladstone to give lodgers the vote, he accepted it from a *radical* Liberal MP, W. T. Torrens. He supported an amendment giving the vote to compounders – householders who paid rates through their landlords – when it came from another radical, Grosvenor Hodgkinson, but turned down a similar and more practical proposal introduced by Hugh Childers, a close personal supporter of Gladstone. Disraeli's original bill gave the vote to householders who paid rates and, although he claimed this was a key indicator of citizenship, he then abandoned the principle by accepting that lodgers should vote. How can historians make sense of his actions?

Disraeli's manoeuvres helped achieve a number of personal and party political aims. The Conservatives had a minority of MPs in the House of Commons and would win parliamentary votes if, and only if, they could get some Liberals on their side. If the Liberals united they could turn the Conservatives out and bring in their own parliamentary reform measures. Consequently Disraeli had to keep them split and stop them all uniting behind Gladstone, their leader in the Commons. Often the only way to do this was to work with radicals by supporting more drastic reform proposals than the Liberal leaders themselves wanted. If Disraeli could manage this – and he did manage it – he could expect to succeed the aged Lord Derby as Conservative leader; show that the Conservatives, who had been out of office for almost all the previous 20 years, were able to govern; and ensure that the Conservatives at least kept some control over the terms of reform. If the Liberals returned to power they were certain to reintroduce reform and could ensure that the details benefited themselves.

Disraeli and his Conservative followers made spectacular concessions by allowing far more voters in the *boroughs*, but the boroughs were largely Liberal anyway. Did it matter much if Liberal MPs were chosen by far more urban electors? Conservatives did best in the counties, the areas outside the boroughs; here Disraeli's bill gave the vote to far fewer people and strengthened the Tory position by ensuring more town residents voted in the boroughs rather than the counties. It was not just the type of voters but how the *constituencies* were divided up that determined who held power, and here the Conservatives made gains. The boundary commissioners who did the dividing were predominantly Tory country gentlemen. They extended borough boundaries to include more suburbs and ensured that the mainly rural south and west were over-represented in comparison with the more industrial north and Midlands. The boundary changes were small but clearly helped the Tories. In the 66 seats where alterations took place, the Tories made a net gain of 25 at the next election, in 1868.

Faced with a seemingly impossible situation, Disraeli apparently won the parliamentary battle by using Liberal splits. Yet Liberal radicals and Conservative right wingers both questioned who was being used and who really won. One radical MP, James Clay, had argued that allowing the Conservatives to stay in office made them more 'squeezable' – they would be likely to make more concessions towards reform than if they were in opposition. Radicals squeezed a lot out of the Conservatives, and it was the Liberals who won the 1868 general election.

Qualifications to vote under the 1867–68 Reform Acts (The Scottish and Irish acts were passed in 1868)

	Boroughs	Proportion of population who could vote	Counties	Proportion of population who could vote
England and Wales	Householders who paid rates; and £10 lodgers (men in lodgings for which they paid at least £10 rent a year) if they had been resident at least a year	English boroughs 1:8 Welsh boroughs 1:8	40-shilling freeholders; copyholders and long leaseholders paying at least £5 rent a year and property holders who paid poor rates and whose land had a rateable value of £12 a year	English counties 1:15 Welsh counties 1:13
Scotland	Householders who paid rates (lodgers had already been able to vote in Scotland as they had legal status as tenants)	1:9	Same as in England	1:24
Ireland	Men occupying property which officials calculating poor rates reckoned was worth £4 rent a year	1:16	Men occupying property which officials calculating poor rates reckoned was worth £12 rent a year	1:26

Notes
1. The general division of constituencies was similar to that after the First Reform Act, but 52 MPs were taken away from small or corrupt boroughs and given to counties and large towns. The voting qualifications in Ireland remained the same as under an act of 1850 except that the sum for the value of borough property was reduced from £8 to £4 a year.
2. The proportions of the population who could vote are taken from F. B. Smith, *The making of the Second Reform Bill*. Cambridge, 1966, p. 239.

The results of reform

How far did the Second Reform Act go to make the United Kingdom a democracy? The exact increase in the electorate is impossible to measure as there are no complete national figures for the general elections before and after the act, in 1865 and 1868. Historians have estimated that the English and Welsh borough electorate grew by 134 per cent and the county one by only 46 per cent – an increase which averaged out over the two countries at about 89 per cent. About a third of adult men could vote. There were separate acts for Scotland and Ireland in 1868. In Scotland the proportion who could vote was a little lower. In Ireland an act of 1850 had already trebled the electorate, but there was little further increase in 1868; only about one-fifth of adult men could vote. (See table above.)

There were great geographical differences, but there was still a big change in how the vote was distributed, even if it was the result of tactical compromise rather than overall planning. Before 1867 the vote was given very much as a privilege, though there were many ways in which men might qualify. Leading politicians began the reform debate by arguing about who was rich, virtuous or educated enough to vote; they ended by giving the right to all borough householders.

The vote now looked more like a general right than a special privilege. If householders in boroughs could vote, why not householders in counties? If unskilled or illiterate men could vote, why not more able women? There was much less controversy about the next two reform acts, which came in 1884 and 1918, than there had been about the first and second. Politicians still argued and manoeuvred, but it became more and more difficult to resist the reasoning behind reform. After the Second Reform Act further change seemed logical.

The ballot and the conduct of elections

The 1868 election which followed the act was the first one in which a majority of borough electors were *working class* and the only one when this working-class majority voted openly. The new voters were easily influenced by employers and landlords, and there was now a much stronger case for a secret ballot. Lord Hartington, who chaired a parliamentary committee investigating election conduct, calculated that the supporters of the secret ballot grew from a small band of advanced radicals before the 1868 election to include most Liberals and Conservatives after it. One of the arguments for open voting was that the electors were voting on behalf of the whole community as some sort of trustees and everyone should see their choice, but this seemed irrelevant if most men in a town had the vote.

The secret ballot was introduced in 1872 and, together with a rule in the 1867 Second Reform Act ending the public nomination of candidates, did much to reduce the violence and street theatre associated with elections. It probably also stopped employers and landlords threatening their workers and tenants, although some doubts remained about how secretly the votes were counted. It did not stop bribery. Commissioners investigating a by-election at Sandwich in 1880 reported that the secret ballot did not appear to have 'the slightest effect in checking bribery. On the contrary, while it enabled many voters to take bribes on both sides, it did not . . . render a single person unwilling to bribe for fear of bribery in vain.'

The exposure of extensive bribery in a few boroughs at the 1880 election provided a strong case for the 1883 Corrupt and Illegal Practices Act. Earlier acts designed to stop candidates buying votes with food, drink and money had little impact, but the 1883 act effectively limited the amount of money and the number of paid workers candidates could use. The reduction of officially recorded election expenditure by three-quarters at the general election in 1885 and the rapid fall in the number of election petitions complaining about corruption have convinced historians that the 1883 act worked. Electoral bribery and violence became the exception rather than the rule, but what had once been common practice would not immediately disappear.

Mid-nineteenth-century election violence was often serious. A Conservative voter had been kicked to death by Irish navvies at Blackburn in 1868, and there was large-scale street fighting. The Tory party had carts of stones in readiness, blood flowed and local schools were used as hospitals. This was exceptional, but in 1868 *The Times* described election nomination days where 'heads are broken' and 'blood flows from numerous noses'. Occasional violence continued at elections until 1885, and was much more widespread in Ireland. Trains leaving Waterford City were said to be full of 'respectable voters' escaping disorder in the town during a by-election campaign in 1870.

Violent habits continued to the end of the nineteenth century. When Rider Haggard stood as a Conservative candidate in East Norfolk in 1895, opposition went beyond the heckling he expected. Three of his meetings broke up in disorder. At one village he was pelted with eggs, and he and his wife got used to coming out of village halls to booing and occasional stone throwing. A little of the old traditions continued into the twentieth century. Even in 1906 systematic bribery was discovered at Worcester, and despite extra police there was street fighting at Barnstaple in Devon accompanied by the kind of excitement 'strongly reminiscent of Barnstaple Fair – only more so'.[2]

Reform in 1884–1885

Why did reform come in 1884–1885?

The Third Reform Act of 1884–85 followed logically from the second. It might be argued that townspeople were more likely to see newspapers and be politically aware than country people, but the distinction soon appeared unreasonable. Many boroughs included villages where agricultural labourers voted; the counties included medium-sized towns and about half a million coal miners who seemed more like industrial than rural workers. Boundaries between counties and boroughs sometimes ran down a street, which meant men on one side missing out on a vote while men opposite voted.

These oddities arose from politicians' tactics in 1867, and they were to be altered when political leaders decided to act. Extending the vote to people in the counties on the same terms as those in the boroughs became the Liberal leader's policy in 1877. Gladstone, who led the 1880–85 Liberal government, supported it in his 1880 election address, and radicals within the Liberal government and parliamentary party pushed for it. Gladstone, as prime minister, decided on the timing. By 1884 his government, bogged down in various Irish and imperial problems, needed some success to show to the voters at home, and he believed his troublesome Liberal party was best managed by getting it to unite behind some major reform. Radicals, like Joseph Chamberlain within the government, favoured giving the vote to all adult men, but Gladstone decided it should just be extended to householders and lodgers paying £10 a year in rent in the counties on the same basis as in the boroughs.

The Conservatives were likely to lose out electorally through the reform as their hold on the English counties would be threatened when the existing electorate of landowners and more substantial tenants was outnumbered by wage-earning workers. Their leaders decided that it was better to compromise and try to manage the new electorate than to mount an unsuccessful and apparently unreasonable fight against change. The passage of reform in 1884–85 had some of the same features as the more epic struggles of 1831–32 and 1866–67. The Conservative majority in the House of Lords blocked the extension of the vote until a scheme for redrawing constituencies was agreed between the party leaderships to ensure that the Liberals did not gain too great a partisan advantage. Gladstone called for dignified demonstrations after the Lords rejection of his bill, and 100,000 working men from nearby counties gave up a day's wages to march through London.

New constituency divisions

The details of the new constituencies were decided largely by negotiation between the party leaders when radical left wingers and the Conservative leader Lord Salisbury both saw advantage in replacing the old system of constituencies which normally elected two MPs by a new one with constituencies electing a single member. The radicals saw this as a logical way of ensuring each MP was chosen by roughly equal numbers of people, a step towards democracy. Salisbury saw it as a way of ensuring that the Conservatives got more MPs, particularly when large towns were divided up and *middle-class* suburban constituencies were created with what he called 'a great deal of villa Toryism'.

The results of reform in 1884–1885

For the first time electoral qualifications were the same in all areas, and a single reform act applied to the whole United Kingdom. Equal treatment for Ireland meant the electorate there rose from about 200,000 to 700,000. With all householders voting and a more uniform pattern of constituencies, election contests became normal for most parliamentary seats and the new system looked something like a democracy for men; the female majority of the population was excluded. Yet in all kinds of ways it was not democratic, and that did much to determine the politics of the next 30 years.

Who could vote? How many times could they vote?

The numbers registered to vote generally fluctuated around 63–66 per cent of all adult men and, allowing for some people having several votes, this meant that only around 60 per cent were electors. Calculations for 1911 show that about 12 per cent of men were excluded because they were not householders. These included servants living with their employers, soldiers in barracks and adult sons who still lived with their families. Most people left off the register were excluded because they had not been living in their homes long enough. An elector had to live in an area for a year before he could go on the register, which did not come into force for another 6 months, so moving house often meant 18 months to 2 years without a vote. In addition, although lodgers who paid £10 rent were entitled to a vote by law, it was so difficult for them to become registered that most apparently failed to do so.

Some historians have suggested that it was mainly working-class voters who lost out through these restrictions, but most of the men left off the register were people who had moved. Many young middle-class men as well as working-class ones moved around and took lodgings, so the procedure stopped younger and more mobile men from voting rather than discriminating against the working class as a whole.

If the working class did not obviously lose out, the wealthy certainly gained by having more than one vote. There were a number of ways in which men could get an extra vote – by having studied at one of the five universities with the right to elect MPs, or by occupying or owning property away from their homes – and men could have an unlimited number of votes. It is estimated that there were at least half a million plural voters in 1911 and that their votes probably counted for about 7 per cent of the total.

What effects did the new constituency divisions have?

The new system was also undemocratic because of the different size of constituencies. The population of the largest was now only 8 times that of the smallest, instead of 250 times as before the reform, but that still left a large difference. Under the so-called first-past-the-post system, where the candidate with most votes wins, gaining power depends largely on the size of the constituencies and how different types of electors are divided between them. Under the 1885 scheme boundaries were to be drawn with reference to the 'pursuits of the people', which meant collecting similar types of voters together, and how these were collected would have a big effect on the outcome of elections.

Key features of the politics of 1885–1914 were closely connected with these arrangements. The Irish Question dominated political life in much of the period, partly at least because of the 101 Irish MPs in the Commons – almost double the number Ireland might have expected if the rules for constituency redistribution had been applied equally there. By the early twentieth century the average Irish seat had around half as many voters as the average English one. The Irish Nationalists gained about 2½ per cent of the total UK vote but over 12 per cent of the seats at Westminster.

The Conservatives dominated British politics from 1886 to 1905, largely because the Irish Question split the Liberals, but also because of their success in large British towns previously won by their opponents. Looking carefully at the 'pursuits of the people', boundary commissioners in 1885 carved out mainly middle-class seats in the suburbs – like Hallam and Eccleshall, which the Conservatives won at Sheffield. The central commercial area of a big city often formed another separate constituency in which the result might be largely influenced by the votes which businessmen living in the suburbs gained from their shops, offices and warehouses. In this way the City of London became the safest Conservative seat in the country and the Conservatives won Central Sheffield.

Different parties might benefit from the distribution according to circumstances, and the constituency divisions had a crucial effect on electoral success. A party which had a modest lead in votes could get a massive majority over other parties in the House of Commons; in 1906 the Liberals had 49 per cent of the vote but 400 out of 670 seats.

The growth of party organisation

Political parties needed a new type of organisation for a new and enlarged electorate after 1867. In the mid-nineteenth century parties generally had a central organisation in London which managed finance and tried to ensure parliamentary candidates were available around the country. Local organisations, like Liberal registration associations, were normally run by wealthy men who concentrated on getting party supporters registered as voters and fighting elections as they arose.

By the early 1870s a different type of local party was fast developing. Research on Lancashire towns shows a growth of working-class clubs which provided a full social life for their members mixed with political propaganda. Members could play billiards, enjoy concerts, eat teas, read newspapers or go on railway excursions, all laid on by their local Liberal or Conservative club. In 1872, for example, the Broughton branch of the Salford Liberal Association moved to new accommodation to provide its members with a 'billiard room . . . reading room, smoke room, chess, draughts, a good supply of papers and periodicals, and the opportunity for obtaining tea, coffee, cigars etc.'. Wolverhampton Liberals held a 'fete and demonstration' including fireworks and an act by 'Zampi the one legged gymnast' for 5,000 people in 1890. Local party organisations even looked after their sick and buried their dead, like the Bolton Conservative Sick and Burial Society, which had been founded in 1848 and expanded after 1867. Politicians hoped that clubs would make people more aware of politics and increase their electoral support. As the mayor of Rochdale put it to local Liberal members, 'with the aid of books and newspapers . . . at their command, they might be better able to discharge those important and responsible duties which the Government . . . had placed in their hands'.[3]

Electoral influence

The clubs were a feature of town life in the 1870s. Politics in the countryside was much more traditional, and landowners kept much of their old influence. In 1883, 11 years after the introduction of the secret ballot, a new book, *The land laws*, by Sir Frederick Pollock mentioned how a tenant's 'political support of the landlord is not unfrequently reckoned on with as much confidence as the performance of the covenants and conditions of the tenancy itself'. Employers still retained a lot of power in small towns, where their workforce might form a large proportion of the electorate after the Second Reform Act. In the small Essex borough of Maldon E. H. Bentall was apparently elected in 1868 because he employed many voters in his agricultural implement works and his opponent threatened to start a rival factory as an electioneering tactic. Even after the secret ballot was introduced wealthy men often kept their influence, and candidates were expected to contribute to local charities when they were not expected to bribe individual voters.

It was more difficult for wealthy men to keep control in large towns. There is very differing evidence about employer influence in big northern factory towns, and it was in these sorts of places that there was more need for party political organisations and clubs.

Conservative and Liberal organisations

After losing the 1868 general election the Conservatives seem to have organised fastest. By 1874, 59 per cent of all English and Welsh constituencies had Conservative associations or Conservative working men's associations. Many were joined up in the National Union started in 1867. This activity helped to lead to Conservative victory at the 1874 general election; 65 out of the 74 English and Welsh constituencies where they won seats from the Liberals had local Conservative associations. In 1877 the Liberals replied with the National Liberal Federation, and by the 1880s both parties had organisations in almost every constituency linked in a national framework.

The overall pattern of organisation was the same in both parties, but the approach was often different. Conservative leaders in London generally worked through wealthy and influential local supporters, persuading them to take the initiative in developing a party association. As a Liberal opponent put it, the party worked 'from above downwards', and Conservative leaders expected their party members to give support, not shape policy. Local Liberal parties often sprang from the existing enthusiasm and organisation of local *Nonconformists*; the National Liberal Federation, in turn, developed from a range of Nonconformist-led pressure groups, particularly the National Education League. Joseph Chamberlain, who took the main initiative in starting the National Liberal Federation, intended it both to win elections and provide a way in which ordinary members could influence policy. Hence there was a complex system of elections and large committees within the federation and its local associations. In theory this allowed ordinary Liberals to feed ideas to their leaders, though opponents claimed that in practice a small number of organisers controlled the whole apparatus. They nick-named it the 'caucus' after the groups of powerful and often corrupt wire-pullers who seemed to dominate American politics.

Whatever its undemocratic features, the National Liberal Federation helped the Liberals gain success in the 1880 and 1885 elections, but it was the Conservatives who had the most professional organisation at the end of the nineteenth century. From 1885 their principal agent, 'Captain' Middleton, developed a very modern type of party machine with a network of professional agents in half the constituencies by 1900.

The Conservatives also had an advantage over the Liberals in the attitude of their supporters and the kind of fringe organisations around the parties. Liberal members were frequently involved in Nonconformist-led organisations concerned with temperance, attacking *Anglican* church privileges or some other special cause. They wanted to use the Liberal party as a vehicle to achieve their group aims and, since their causes or 'fads' varied a lot, it was often difficult to avoid disagreement and get much sense of common purpose. Conservatives, on the other hand, seemed much more willing to rally behind their leaders and what they saw as the cause of their country and empire. Their main fringe organis-ation, the Primrose League – started in 1883 and named after Disraeli's favourite flower – soon grew to over a million members in 1891 and 2 million by 1910. Its members concentrated on tea parties and entertainments rather than trouble-some and divisive political priorities, but they readily accepted upper-class social and political leadership and often worked for the party at election times.

Election campaigns and national issues

How far were British elections now about local or national issues? How far did men see themselves voting for constituency candidates or national party leaders? Local issues and personalities often seemed more important than national ones after the Second Reform Act, and the continuing influence of landlords and employers illustrates this. Yet the growth of national party organisations was one of several developments which gradually altered the situation.

The high-profile battle between Gladstone and Disraeli from 1867 to 1880 helped focus electors' minds on national issues, and Gladstone particularly had great popular appeal. Tickets for his speech at Birmingham to launch the National Liberal Federation in 1877 cost 5 shillings (25p) – the equivalent of something like a day's wages for an ordinary working man – and yet the hall holding about 10,000 people could apparently have been filled four times over. In many ways the 1880 election was the first modern campaign, with two national party organisations and speaking tours by party leaders.

Gladstone won publicity by fighting a by-election campaign in Midlothian in late 1879, and Conservative leaders in the government then had to reply. The *Annual Register* reckoned that during the 1879 recess – the break between parliamentary sessions – and in the run up to the general election 'more speeches had been made by Cabinet ministers than in all the recesses of other parliaments put together'. Disraeli restricted his speech-making outside parliament to a few addresses in his own constituency and a few great performances to party rallies. Salisbury, the next Conservative leader, spoke outside parliament over seventy times during 1881–85.

The 1883 Corrupt and Illegal Practices Act subsequently increased the importance of party organisation by restricting what individual candidates could spend. Campaigning could still be colourful and individualistic. Rider Haggard, standing in East Norfolk in 1895, held 'smoking concerts' where his friend Arthur Cochrane sang popular music-hall songs like 'The baby on the shore' before he himself gave a political speech. Generally, though, as candidates were often prevented from hiring as many helpers as they wanted, they relied more on volunteer party workers who often felt a loyalty to national leaders. As less could be spent in each constituency, the parties raised more money centrally to spend on a national campaign.

Newspapers provided voters with more and more of their information about parties. Nationally newspaper circulation is estimated to have been 30 times higher in 1870 than in 1830. The trend continued, and total daily newspaper readers are estimated to have quadrupled from 1896 to 1914. The provincial press expanded rapidly in the later nineteenth century; 16 English towns had a daily paper in 1868 and 71 in 1901. Even local and regional papers would often give lengthy reports on parliamentary debates and party leaders' speeches, and the national press was developing fast. The best-selling daily newspaper – the *Daily Telegraph* – sold 190,0000 copies in 1870, but a new, more popular type of paper began with the *Daily Mail* in 1896. In the early twentieth century it sold around three-quarters to a million copies. Other popular papers followed, such as the *Daily Mirror*, which also sold a million in 1912. These papers did not report top politicians' speeches fully, as the more traditional ones did, but they gave summaries and reached far more people. The growth in central party organisation together with the higher profile of party leaders and wider reading of London newspapers produced more of a countrywide general election campaign, but were electors voting on a clear set of national party policies?

Today an elected government is expected to carry out the policies in its election manifesto; gaining a majority in the House of Commons is said to give party leaders a mandate (an instruction or authorisation from the voters) to do what they have promised. The two main parties did not issue national manifestos setting out detailed policies before the First World War. Party leaders issued a personal appeal to the electorate, sent out specifically to their own constituency if they sat in the House of Commons, but they did not see this as a complete statement of party policy or a formal agreement with the electorate. Gladstone was keen to get support for his policies from the voters but did not see himself as getting a mandate or instructions from them. In practice politicians argued that clear approval for a policy from the electorate justified a government in pushing it through, but that they were not obliged to ask the voters. Gladstone claimed that voters had given him specific support to disestablish the Church of Ireland after he fought the 1868 election on the issue and, on the other side, Salisbury suggested the House of Lords should reject the secret ballot in 1872 as the electorate had not voted for it. In 1886 Gladstone introduced a vital bill to give Home Rule in Ireland, although Liberal leaders had not put it forward as a policy in the general election five months earlier. Gladstone thought the claim that voters should have been asked 'an extraordinary doctrine, I want to know where it is to be found in any Constitutional authority'.

In the 1880s Joseph Chamberlain was the Liberal politician who seemed most enthusiastically in favour of democratic control and of presenting such a programme to the electorate. In 1873 he had suggested that the way of uniting the Liberal party was to 'choose out the most important of all the questions debated, and weld them into a connected scheme which all or most of us may accept as our programme'. Yet by 1886 Chamberlain wanted to avoid too specific commitments to the voters so that politicians were able to develop a strong empire: 'The problem is to give democracy the whole power, but to induce them to do no more in the way of using it than to decide on the general principles which they wish to see carried out and the men by whom they are to be carried out.'[4]

In 1891 Gladstone accepted resolutions at the National Liberal Federation Conference at Newcastle which seemed to make up a kind of programme, but he did not present these as his manifesto at the general election the next year. Although the Liberals clearly fought to maintain free trade in 1906, to pass their people's budget in January 1910 and to reform the House of Lords in December 1910, the main parties' policies were still publicised in a mass of leaflets from their central organisations and addresses from individual candidates rather than in a single national manifesto.

Local government and elections

Political parties and clubs were concerned with fighting local elections as well as national ones. A succession of boards and councils set up to meet different needs (see Chapter 5) were generally elected by ratepayers, and even some tenants who did not pay rates could vote from 1869. On the other hand, wealthy men might have up to six votes for electing different boards according to the property they owned until changes in 1894. Elections for these boards and councils were often the main political concerns of party branches in towns. School board elections begun from 1870 were often hard fought because they were normally about religious issues. There was a divide between the Conservative party supporting the Anglicans, and local Liberal groups which were often led by strong Nonconformists.

County councils were established in 1888 and parish councils in 1894, in addition to existing borough councils and various boards like the poor law guardians. In 1894 urban and rural district councils took over a number of jobs from different authorities. These and the parish councils were then elected by all those who already had council and parliamentary votes through occupying property. There were party political contests for only a minority of county council seats at the start, but council elections generally became more political in the following years. Salisbury urged Conservatives to make the London County Council elections in 1894 'a party fight', and independent Labour party groups became involved in many town council elections from the 1890s.

Landowners in politics

Continuing landowner power was strongly connected with the start of county councils in 1888. Previously the country areas outside the scope of borough councils had been substantially administered by local *magistrates* (*Justices of the Peace* or *JPs*), and about three-quarters came from landed families. Slightly over half the newly elected county councillors were also magistrates. Many magistrates who had chaired the old quarter sessions running the counties also chaired the new county councils, and often little seemed to have changed. In some counties local *aristocrats* – like the Fifth Marquess of Bath, who was chairman of Wiltshire County Council from 1904 to 1945 – helped to preside over county government for years to come, but there was a long-term shift to business and professional people running the councils rather than landowners.

There was a considerable reduction of landowner power in parliamentary elections after the Third Reform Act of 1884–85, with a new mass county electorate and redistribution of seats from small boroughs to large towns. The Conservative party – the main pillar of landed power – was changing as more of its members came from urban constituencies, and from 1885 most new Conservative MPs came from middle-class families. With an accompanying reduction in landowner numbers in the Liberal party, their mid-nineteenth-century dominance in the House of Commons declined. Whereas about three-quarters of MPs had come from landed families in 1865, around half did in 1885–86 and under a third in 1900.

In Ireland there was a swift change after the electorate was more than tripled under the Third Reform Act. Few landowners remained as MPs and few were elected to Irish county councils when they were established in 1898.

In Britain landowners often remained as county MPs and more frequently played a major part in running local constituency parties. Nevertheless, with economic problems in farming from the 1890s, many landowners found increasing difficulty in meeting all the expenses of being an MP, especially as they were expected to make contributions to local charities and pay many of their election expenses. Some disliked the new type of politics in which they increasingly had to act as servants to the electorate. Bertram Freeman-Mitford explained why he gave up after three years as a Conservative MP: 'I was perfectly determined not to stand again . . . Primrose League meetings, bazaars, political gatherings in schoolrooms, attended perhaps by a dozen yokels, 2 or 3 women and a little boy . . . made life impossible.'

In the cabinet the change in social composition was gradual, but there was a slow shift from a landowning to a middle-class majority among ministers around the start of the twentieth century. By 1914 even most British county MPs were no longer from the traditional landed class. The payment of MPs agreed in 1911 made it easier for working men to enter parliament. A gradual but massive change was taking place in the type of people who held power in the UK government.

Women and the vote

Why did women not have the vote?

The parliamentary electorate before the First World War contained about 60 per cent of men, but under 30 per cent of the whole population. In many ways it is hard to explain why women did not have the vote in general elections. It was not a matter of tradition; women who met the property qualification had voted in parliamentary and local elections up to the early nineteenth century, and they were specifically excluded by the First Reform Act in 1832 and the Municipal Corporations Act in 1835. Nor did it really reflect their place in society, although there was much discrimination against them in Victorian Britain. Married women had won property rights by acts of 1870–82, and women gained entry to various professions. Not only did they have a vote in local municipal council elections from 1869 if they were ratepayers, but large numbers were also elected to local councils, school boards and boards of poor law guardians. By 1914 over 3,000 had been members of these bodies over the past 45 years, and there were a few women mayors.

Although both Conservative and Liberal leaders were divided over votes for women, the Conservative prime minister Lord Salisbury said he was converted to it 'in principle' in 1890–91, and the Conservative Party Conference passed resolutions in favour of it before 1900. A majority in the House of Commons approved bills for women's suffrage (voting rights) on several occasions from 1884 to 1911. About half the members of the Conservative Primrose League were women; the Liberal and Labour parties had their own women's organisations, and women participated in election campaigns. Why did women not get the parliamentary vote?

The first issue was whether the vote should be extended to women on the same terms as men, which meant giving it to a minority of women holding property. This would mean many single women voting, but very few married ones. It was also thought that this would benefit wealthy women disproportion-ately, which encouraged Conservative support for it but worried the Liberal leaders who were in government from 1905 to the First World War. Both David Lloyd George and Winston Churchill gave it as a reason for opposing women's suffrage bills. Extending the vote to all adult men and women might be the democratic answer, but it would be a massive change. Conservative MPs who were prepared to support an extension of the vote to women on the same terms as men would be less likely to accept it, and it would mean suddenly going from a position where no women voted to a female majority in the electorate.

There was also the practical problem of how a law granting women the vote would be passed through parliament. The Commons gave approval to bills introduced by individual MPs – private members' bills – but, given the way parliamentary business was organised, a bill introduced by the government stood a much better chance of becoming law. Achieving government sponsorship was difficult because the issue was so divisive in both political parties, and there were party political reasons for Liberal ministers to be apprehensive about giving the vote to women on the same terms as men.

Although *suffragist* and *suffragette* groups in favour of giving women the vote attracted a lot of attention, there was an anti-suffragist movement with a number of effective arguments. The main one was the idea of 'separate spheres' – that women's area of activity, the home and bringing up children, was quite different from men's, which involved outside work, public affairs and therefore political life. The idea was not wholly realistic in Victorian and Edwardian Britain. The 1911 census showed that 55 per cent of single women and 14 per cent of married women were in paid employment, and they made up around 30 per cent of the labour force, but the thinking involved was accepted by not only men but also many women.

As Britain was a small nation trying to control a much larger population in its empire, many saw maintenance of imperial defence as a government's first priority. They often argued that because women were unable to fight and were too emotional, they would not defend the empire properly if they were in government (see Document 2.2). Since Britain's first woman prime minister, Margaret Thatcher, was criticised for her domineering manner and successfully led a war to defend one of Britain's last colonies, the Falklands, this argument now sounds absurd, but it seemed very important around 1900 when some of the most enthusiastic imperialists, like Lord Curzon and Joseph Chamberlain, were also strongly opposed to women's suffrage.

Above all, giving women the vote and eventually getting a female majority in the electorate meant entering a different political world. Right wingers often saw a threat to tradition and national strength. Left wingers sometimes feared that women concerned about security and home life might be a conservative force in the electorate. Active 'suffragists' were a small minority among women; did men really have to enter a new and unknown world of equality of the sexes in politics?

The campaign for women's votes

Suffragist organisations had to persuade men that they did have to accept change. A series of women's suffrage groups developed from the 1860s and amalgamated in 1897 into the National Union of Women's Suffrage Societies led by Mrs Millicent Fawcett. These so-called suffragist organisations were non-violent and campaigned in legal ways. Their arguments through pamphlets and meetings may have helped win a majority for women's voting rights in several Commons divisions, but progress was slow and unspectacular.

In 1903 Mrs Emmeline Pankhurst founded the Women's Social and Political Union (WSPU) – generally known as the suffragettes – to develop higher-profile campaigning using large demonstrations and disrupting political meetings. Whereas the National Union tried to increase support for the private members' bills introduced by individual MPs to give women voting rights, the WSPU was more concerned to pressurise the government by whipping up public opinion and persuading or intimidating ministers. They interrupted Liberal ministers' speeches and later turned to more violent methods, which included breaking shop windows, setting light to pillar boxes, putting a firebomb in the chancellor of the exchequer's house and, in the case of Emily Davison, suicide by walking into the horses running in the 1913 Derby.

The effect of this on the women's cause is a matter of controversy. At first some women belonged to both a non-violent suffragist organisation and the more militant suffragette one. Large suffragette demonstrations attracted publicity and seem to have achieved more in a short time than the more peaceful, dispassionate approach of the National Union. By drawing attention to the women's franchise issue they apparently led more people to join the National Union, whose membership increased from 12,000 to over 50,000 from 1909 to 1914. The suffragette movement also raised increasing quantities of money, showing the commitment it inspired; its income rose from £2,700 in 1907 to £36,500 by 1914. However, the suffragettes could also be counter-productive once they were using violence as a key weapon to pressurise the public. Opponents used suffragette tactics as examples illustrating that women were too emotional and unbalanced to vote, and politicians did not want to give in to a kind of terrorism.

Parliament and women's votes

For several years up to 1912 the House of Commons voted for conciliation bills to grant women the vote on the same terms as men – bills drawn up by supporters of women's suffrage from different parties united in a so-called conciliation committee. In 1912 and 1913 similar bills for women's suffrage were defeated. This was partly because the Liberal government had introduced a bill in 1912 to extend the vote to all adult men. An extension of the vote to all adult women, which then seemed likely if a conciliation bill were passed, would be very different from the original proposal and fewer MPs were prepared to support it. The defeats were partly due to reduced support among some Irish Nationalist and Labour MPs for tactical reasons and because of absences which were not really connected with the suffrage issue. Yet some MPs and ministers did apparently turn against the bills because of the suffragette campaign. Sydney Buxton, the president of the Board of Trade, wrote to *The Times* explaining his change of mind on the issue: 'I feel convinced that to pass the Bill just now might appear to be, and would undoubtedly be claimed by the militants and their admirers to be, a justification for and an endorsement by the House of Commons of their methods and actions.' Millicent Fawcett, the suffragist leader, told the newspapers that the suffragette militants were 'the chief obstacles in the way of the success of the suffrage movement in the House of Commons and far more formidable opponents of it than Mr Asquith or Mr Harcourt [the leading anti-suffragist ministers in the government]'. The suffragette movement drew attention to the women's cause brilliantly, but did it actually delay them from getting the vote?

Contrasting ideas on female suffrage

2.1 The case for women's voting rights

The suffragette leader, Mrs Emmeline Pankhurst, in 1908

it is important that women should have the vote in order that in the government of the country the women's point of view should be put forward . . . [An MP's] time is fully taken up by attending to the needs of the people who have sent him to Parliament . . . you cannot take up a newspaper, you cannot go to a conference, you cannot even go to church, without hearing a great deal of talk about social reform and a demand for social legislation. Of course, it is obvious that that kind of legislation – and the Liberal Government tell us that if they remain in office long enough we are going to have a great deal of it – is of vital importance to women . . . We are hearing about legislation to decide what kind of homes people are to live in. That surely is a question for women . . . Since 1870 men have been trying to find out how to educate children. I think they have not yet realised that if they are ever to find out how to educate children, they will have to take women into their confidence . . .

Source: 'The importance of the vote', a lecture given at the Portman Rooms, London, 24 March 1908

2.2 The case against women's voting rights

Lord Curzon, a leading Conservative opponent of women's suffrage, in 1912

The whole life of the working man is a political school. The papers which he reads every day, the public meetings which he attends, the debating societies to which many belong, the enormous influence of the Press – all of these are a mechanism for familiarizing the working man with his duties . . . it is a different question when you come to women . . .

Issues sometimes arise in public affairs – you can see them on the horizon now – great issues of peace and war, of treaties and alliances, of the treatment to be adopted to our Colonies and dependencies. An unwise, and still more an emotional, decision of those issues might in circumstances which it is easy to imagine lead to the disruption and even to the ruin of the Empire . . . Suppose that it was a question of instituting national compulsory military training in this country. I ask you, are those the sort of questions that in a reflective mood you would wish to be decided by a majority of women? . . .

What is the good of talking about the equality of the sexes? The first whiz of the bullet, the first boom of the cannon, and where is the equality of the sexes? When it comes to fighting, war has to be decided, always has been decided, and always will be decided, by one sex alone.

Source: D. M. Chapman-Huston (ed.), *Subjects of the day: selection of speeches and writings by Earl Curzon of Kedleston*, London, 1915, pp. 301–04

2.3 A postcard against women's voting rights (1905)

2.4 A postcard and poster in favour of women's voting rights (1912)

Document case-study questions

1 How do Documents 2.1 and 2.2 present different arguments about women's suffrage by stressing different government responsibilities?

2 What is the argument of Document 2.3 and what attitudes from the Edwardian period does it illustrate? Think about the idea of separate spheres and to which social class the postcard refers.

3 How effectively do Documents 2.1 and 2.4 counter the arguments against women's suffrage in Document 2.2?

4 How useful are these documents in explaining the bitterness and violence which accompanied the struggle for women's rights in the period 1905–14?

Notes and references

1 M. Cowling, *Disraeli, Gladstone and revolution*, Cambridge, 1967; R. J. Harrison, *Before the socialists: studies in labour and politics, 1861–1881*, London, 1965.

2 *Western Times*, 27 January 1906, quoted in M. Dawson, 'Liberalism in Devon and Cornwall: "the old time religion"', *Historical Journal*, June 1995.

3 J. Garrard, 'Parties, members and voters after 1867', in T. R. Gourvish and A. O'Day (eds.), *Later Victorian Britain 1867–1900*, London, 1988.

4 J. L. Garvin, *Life of Joseph Chamberlain*, vol. 2, London, 1933, p. 191.

The apparent achievement of democracy

The vote was extended to all adult men and most women by a reform act in 1918; women only gained the vote on equal terms under further legislation in 1928. The distribution of MPs and the system of voting has a major impact on elections, and there was much discussion about these in 1917–18. National election campaigns developed in more complex ways with the growth of new media.

The Fourth Reform Act, 1918

The Fourth Reform Act of 1918 brought the largest ever increase in the electorate, which went up about two and a half times. It raised the proportion of adult men who voted from around 60 per cent to 95 per cent and gave the vote to most women. This was at least something near democracy. Many historians have seen it as uncontroversial and inevitable, and so did some politicians at the time, but there was a lot of disagreement over details. Like those of other reform acts, its terms resulted from a mixture of national circumstances and politicians' tactics.

Reasons for reform

A general election had been due in 1915 and, although all parties in parliament agreed to put this off, the government still thought it must make plans for elections during wartime. This raised an immediate problem of who would vote. Soldiers hazarding their lives for their country on the Western Front surely deserved a vote, but under existing law they would not get one. They were not on the register, which only included men who had been resident in their homes for over a year. Therefore the registers must be revised, and they could not be drawn up as before because that would exclude the absent soldiers. If the registers were to be compiled in a new way, that meant an immediate reform of voting qualifications, which would be very controversial. The main political parties were managing the war together in a coalition from 1915, but there was much disagreement about what should be done about elections. The way the government chose to work out an agreed reform was to set up a committee of party politicians from the Lords and Commons in 1916, chaired by the Speaker (chairman) of the Commons as an obviously neutral person. This soon became known as the Speaker's Conference, and it agreed on all its recommendations except the way in which the vote would be granted to women.

Why did women get the vote?

There have been two main lines of popular argument to explain why women gained the vote in 1918. One is that the *suffragette* and *suffragist* campaigns before the war produced delayed results. The suffragette campaign had been called off quickly at the outbreak of war. Its leader, Mrs Pankhurst, who believed in using violent methods, took to the recruiting platform. Mrs Fawcett, leader of the non-violent suffragist movement, called on women to show themselves 'worthy of citizenship' even though they had not gained the vote. Some moderate campaigners contacted MPs when the need for voting reform led to the Speaker's Conference in 1916 and during the parliamentary discussions in 1917–18. Maybe the fear of renewed and violent agitation after the war influenced politicians. Lord Crewe referred to a possible revival of militant action in a House of Lords debate in January 1918, but overall this did not come up much in parliamentary discussion. Violence had put some politicians off granting women the vote in 1912; perhaps the absence of aggressive campaigning made it easier to concede it in 1917–18.

The second popular explanation is that women won the vote because of the work they did in the war. When so many women did men's jobs it was difficult to argue against their voting like men. Herbert Asquith, who as prime minister had opposed giving women the vote before the war, made the best-known statement of this argument: 'I think that some years ago I ventured to use the expression "Let the women work out their own salvation." Well, Sir, they have worked it out during this war. How could we have carried on the war without them?'

The terms on which women gained the vote hardly suggest that politicians were following this line of thinking. Large numbers of young women became munitions workers or land girls, and yet only women over 30 gained the vote in 1918. Wartime needs emphasised men's role as fighters, and the idea of the male breadwinner remained. Women frequently left their new jobs after the war, some were forced out, and the state soon discriminated against married women in government employment, making them give way to men. Voting rights did not accompany equality for women at work.

Perhaps women gaining the vote in 1918 does not require any special explanation. As Chapter 2 suggests, with many women in local government, significant numbers in professional jobs and a large proportion going out to work, the arguments against their voting looked increasingly unreasonable. The MPs who approved women's suffrage in 1918 had largely been elected in 1910, and a majority favoured it then, as shown by a Commons vote in 1911. There was a majority against women voting in 1912 and 1913, but this was because of problems in deciding how many men and women should vote and possibly because of suffragette violence. Many Liberals had feared giving the vote to property-owning women alone, and many Conservatives were worried about giving the vote to every adult. When it was clear that the vote would be granted to almost all adult men anyway because so many of them were soldiers, both Liberals and Conservatives seemed to find it easier to give the vote to women as well – Liberals because the women voters would not be a social elite and Conservatives because the reform seemed increasingly inevitable and was linked to feelings of patriotic solidarity in war.

Conservatives had been very divided before the war over whether any women should vote, but they were more broadly opposed to full adult suffrage, which a Liberal government had tried to introduce for men in 1912. Conservative MPs could be expected to oppose the changes in the Fourth Reform Act, and many did. Four Conservative members resigned from the Speaker's Conference rather than agree to its proposal. Over a hundred Conservative MPs signed a petition against acting on its report after it was published, and 40 then voted against the Reform Bill in parliament, but in the end most Conservative MPs followed their leaders in the coalition government in supporting reform.

Some of the proposals brought advantages for the party, and they gained important concessions. The Conservatives could hope to benefit from the way MPs were redistributed around the country, particularly as there should be fewer MPs for underpopulated nationalist areas of Ireland. The Liberals had tried to stop men having extra votes through property ownership before the war, but these plural votes were partly retained. While Conservatives had often thought that young, propertyless men would generally vote against them, they now thought – probably wrongly – that young soldiers would tend to support them. They also saw that they might get useful amendments to the bill in parliament, as they did. Commissioners deciding on *constituency* boundaries were instructed to allow more MPs in country areas because of their scattered population, and it was easier for some businessmen to get a second vote in towns. Both of these changes were likely to benefit the Conservatives, who saw that they were getting a generally acceptable compromise. There were fears about *working-class* disturbances in 1917–18, and in these circumstances it was best not to risk revolutionary unrest or offend new electors by opposing their right to vote when they were going to get it anyway.

Voting qualifications

The 1918 act was more democratic than earlier ones, and its voting qualifications were simpler than before. Previously men could vote on the basis of seven different voting qualifications which were sometimes difficult to define. Now they could vote just by living in a house – on what is termed a 'residence qualification', rather like the present-day arrangement except that they needed to have lived in a place for six months before they could go onto the electoral register. Women either had to be householders who paid rates or to have husbands who were. People could get a second vote either by having property in a constituency where they did not live or by having studied at a university which had MPs.

The electorate increased from 7.7 million in 1910 to 21.4 million in 1918 – from under 30 per cent of the adult population to around 78 per cent. Over three-quarters of the voters at the 1918 general election had never voted before, and about two-thirds of the new voters were women. It was the largest proportion of new voters ever at a British election.

Effects for women

The new electorate included most women, but they did not get the vote on equal terms with men. They made up 42–43 per cent of the voters, although women's longer lifespan produced a female majority in the population which was more marked because of the three-quarters of a million deaths among British men in the First World War. Politicians did not expect the restrictions on women's voting to last long, but they were not prepared to go straight from a ban on women voting to female dominance. They were ready to have female MPs, and three weeks before the 1918 general election a law gave women the right to stand for parliament. Lady Astor, the first woman MP to take her seat, entered the House of Commons after a by-election in 1919, but women only played a small part in parliamentary life up to 1945 and beyond. Lady Astor stood because her husband, an MP, had inherited a peerage and gone to the House of Lords; she was basically standing in for him and claimed to be carrying on his work. Margaret Bondfield became the first woman cabinet minister as minister of labour in the Labour government of 1929, but there were still few female MPs. The highest number before the Second World War was 14 – 2.3 per cent of the House of Commons – in 1929. By then women made up over 50 per cent of the electorate, but they comprised only about 5 per cent of parliamentary candidates and councillors in the 1930s.

Effects for different classes

Over 35 per cent of men had not previously had the vote, and they made up around a third of the new voters. The proportion of men able to vote had differed greatly from one area to another. It had been particularly low in working-class areas of cities and where people moved frequently. Some historians have seen the Fourth Reform Act as giving the working class voting strength in proportion to their numbers for the first time. People were no longer prevented from voting because they received poor relief, and many working-class servants and soldiers who were not householders gained the vote in 1918.

Some of the previous restrictions on voting may have hit the *middle class* nearly as much as the working class (see p. 25). Because of residence qualifications, moving had generally meant losing the vote for about two years, and many middle-class men moved out of cities to the suburbs or to other areas because of their professions, just as many working-class men changed homes. The six-month residence qualification in 1918 significantly reduced the numbers who lost out; it deprived only about 5 per cent of men of voting rights.

For lodgers, getting on the electoral register had often involved a kind of legal obstacle course, and working-class ones outside London might not have paid the £10 a year rent qualification anyway. Undoubtedly working-class lodgers were less likely to vote than middle-class ones, but research on the Scottish area of East Lothian, which has unusually detailed records from 1911, suggests that many working-class lodgers did vote. If this is representative of Britain as a whole, the system discriminated less against the working class than many historians have supposed. Which lodgers voted often seemed to depend on the work of party agents and officers compiling the election register. At a time when on average men married at about 30 and single men rarely set up their own households, young men frequently could not vote. Estimates from both Conservative Central Office at the time, and historians later, suggest about 450,000 out of 600,000 single middle-class men did not qualify for the lodger vote. Overall, it is unlikely that the old voting qualifications had reduced the working-class proportion of voters by much more than 4–5 per cent,[1] but there is no doubt that wealthier and better educated men benefited from plural voting.

Before 1918 plural votes – the extra votes men had through property ownership or electing university MPs – made up about 7 per cent of the total. Men could vote only once in each constituency, but could do so in an unlimited number of areas if they qualified. From the Fourth Reform Act people could have only one extra vote. Most of these came from ownership of business premises in constituencies where the voter did not live, and there had been approximately half a million votes of this kind before the war. This total was now reduced to about 159,000, just over 1 per cent of the total. There were also an increased number of MPs representing universities, elected by those who had attended them; but they only chose 12 MPs out of 707. The second votes based on wealth and education certainly did not fit in with normal democratic principles, and they lasted only up until 1948.

Distribution of MPs

Voting qualifications were the basis of individual democratic rights, but it was still how MPs were distributed between different areas which decided where power lay. Population changes, particularly the emigration from Ireland and growth of London suburbs, had led to big differences between the electorates of the smallest and largest constituencies. Back at the 1910 elections Kilkenny in southern Ireland had a few hundred voters and Romford in Essex over 50,000. Under the 1918 act a boundary commission was to draw up a new pattern of single-member constituencies with a population of about 70,000, except for twelve moderately large towns which would keep two MPs each. The number of MPs representing outer London suburbs increased from 15 to 40. Since Ireland kept as many MPs as before, it was still strongly over-represented, but this disparity only lasted until 1921 when most of the country became self-governing and only Northern Ireland continued to send representatives to the British parliament. Allowing for some big country constituencies having fewer voters so that they did not extend over too large an area, the United Kingdom was divided up in quite a reasonable way. Geographically the distribution looked fair, but there was more parliamentary discussion about reforming the voting system in 1917–18 than at any other time up to the 1990s.

Different electoral systems

Voters in each constituency choosing a single MP and the person with most votes going to parliament is a straightforward system which may look fair and simple. The most popular individual at the poll represents their own area, and if the number of electors in each constituency is roughly equal it may seem that all are equally represented. There are, however, some strong arguments against this system, normally known as first-past-the-post, being properly representative. Firstly, the candidate with most votes may not have more than half. Where three or four candidates stand in an election the winner may have little more than a third or a quarter of the votes cast and only represent a minority of the electors. This problem can be overcome by an alternative vote (AV) system, in which voters indicate their second, third or further preferences as well as their first choice; second preference votes from losing candidates can then be reallocated until one candidate has more than 50 per cent. This ensures that the winning candidate is in some way the choice of the majority, but it means that second preference votes often count equally with first preference ones.

The second problem with the first-past-the-post system is that when electors are choosing parties rather than individuals the overall result of an election in different constituencies may not be very representative of the overall pattern of voting. If one party keeps winning seats with just over half the votes, it can dominate an elected assembly in a way that scarcely represents voters' wishes, and if candidates win with about 35–40 per cent of the vote, as sometimes happens, a party can get control in an elected parliament while being opposed by a substantial majority of the population.

A party with support from a small minority of the overall population can get fair representation if its electors are concentrated in a few areas, as the Irish Nationalists were in the early twentieth century, but if its support is more evenly distributed it may get few MPs or none despite winning the votes of millions of people. Systems of proportional representation (PR), in which parliamentary seats are allocated between parties over a wider area in proportion to numbers of votes, will produce an assembly which more fairly reflects electors' preferences. The problems in these systems come from their complexity and the lack of control voters may have over how party leaders do deals among themselves.

The Speaker's Conference recommended that some large towns should elect MPs on a PR basis and that other parts of the country should be divided into single-member constituencies with an AV system. These proposals produced more disagreement than the changes in voting qualifications and, while some may have weighed up the theoretical arguments, most MPs and peers seem to have voted according to what they calculated would be best for themselves and their parties. Labour and Liberal MPs generally favoured an AV system as they thought they could benefit from left-wing voters being able to use second preferences, and Conservative MPs opposed it for the same reason. Some Conservatives favoured a PR system in large towns as they thought this would help them if they were in a minority there and many feared growing left-wing influence in the working class. The majority of Conservative MPs reasoned differently and opposed PR, but it was widely supported by Conservative peers. The result was that the House of Commons came out in favour of the AV system; the Lords rejected it and voted for extensive PR. The Lords then suggested a compromise with more limited PR, but since no agreement could be reached on either reform, parliamentarians fell back on the more traditional first-past-the-post as the one acceptable way out. Some think this was what Conservative peers opposed to AV were planning all along.

The cost of elections

The law not only laid down who could vote and how MPs were distributed. It did much to decide on the cost of elections and what campaigns were like. Under the 1918 act local councils had to compile registers of who could vote by sending forms to everybody's home as they do today, so party candidates no longer had to employ people between elections to ensure their supporters were registered. They also no longer had to contribute to the cost of holding elections. Instead they were helped by having the right to send voters an election address free of charge through the Post Office and could use elementary school halls for campaign meetings without paying. The maximum amount candidates could spend on elections was reduced to under half of what it had been before, under the terms of the 1883 Corrupt Practices Act. If they got under an eighth of the votes they would not be entitled to the return of the £150 deposit that all candidates had to pay – a large sum roughly equivalent to a working man's annual income. This deterred many from standing, but major party candidates found elections much cheaper than before.

Effects for political parties

Electoral reforms inevitably change political life, and in different ways the terms of the 1918 act helped produce Conservative dominance before the Second World War. Surveys suggest that the Conservatives gained considerably more support among women than Labour, and they certainly had about four times as many women party members at the end of the 1920s. They held 35 of the 40 seats in the outer London suburbs at all the elections from 1918 up to 1945 and retained several MPs because of plural voting. The business vote won them a few seats in inner cities, and a majority of university MPs were Conservative before 1935.

Several historians have argued that Labour gained most from the Fourth Reform Act, but this is doubtful. The working-class proportion of the electorate probably increased only marginally, and anyway Labour made large gains in local council elections where the voting qualifications were still largely based on householding and had not altered much from before the First World War. Labour candidates may have benefited more than most from having cheaper elections – they normally won enough votes to save their deposits, and finance was a special problem for working-class politicians unless they had trade union money.

Equal voting rights for women, 1928

Women got the vote on equal terms with men in 1928. It was a move towards full democracy which politicians thought logical from 1918, but many saw its timing as a matter of political chance. The Conservative prime minister, Stanley

Baldwin, declared at the previous election, in 1924, that the Conservatives were 'in favour of equal political rights for men and women' and suggested a conference of all political parties to get agreement on reform.

Was this a promise to give the vote to women on the same terms as men before the next general election? Under pressure in the House of Commons during the next year, Baldwin's home secretary, Sir William Joynson-Hicks, said the promise meant 'no difference will take place in the ages at which men and women go to the poll at the next election'. This was more definite and, although the cabinet was divided, it decided to bring in the change. The Conservative leadership suggested that both men and women might vote at 25 but, since that would mean many young men losing the vote, that was soon thought too controversial. Consequently the Conservative government brought in a law in 1928 to give men and women over 21 a vote for parliament and local authorities on equal terms. The government did gain what they saw as one political advantage by giving a further vote to wives or husbands of business voters, which increased second votes based on business property by over a third.

THE JUDGMENT OF GLADYS.

What does this cartoon, published in *Punch* on 21 March 1928, suggest will be the effect on politics of giving younger women the vote and what does this imply about their political attitudes?

Women made up 52.7 per cent of the electorate after the 1928 act – about 10 per cent more than before. The new voters increased the overall number by about 16.5 per cent. Although about a third of these were over 30, politicians and journalists concentrated most on the women in their 20s, frequently referred to as 'flappers' to suggest that they were lighthearted and irresponsible. Middle-aged male journalists often saw young ladies who sometimes smoked, wore short skirts or danced the Charleston as either politically ignorant or worryingly left wing. There seems to be no sound evidence for this whatsoever. Surveys comparing swings between parties at the next election with numbers of new women voters suggest that, if anything, they were more Conservative than the electorate as a whole.

The 1928 act was the last significant electoral reform before the Second World War. A Labour government depending on Liberal support in 1929–31 brought in a bill to abolish plural voting and introduce AV, but it was drastically altered by the House of Lords and the government fell before it could become law.

Party politics and election campaigns

The 1920s and 1930s saw a better organised, more literate and in many ways more professional type of politics, largely dominated by the Conservative party. The trend towards quieter elections seen since the 1870s continued after the First World War. *The Times*'s parliamentary correspondent referred in 1918 to the disappearance of 'street-corner rowdyism, blatant posters . . . fleets of highly-coloured motor cars and carefully managed torchlight processions'. A Cornish newspaper described the 1929 election as 'deadly dull' in contrast to the time when 'every other meeting was an incipient riot'. Candidates still met disorderly election crowds, but they were very unusual.

Politics became more national. This was shown by the development of central party organisations – Conservative Central Office grew from a small unit with only six staff in 1902 to over two hundred in the 1930s. Labour developed a London headquarters on a smaller scale than the Conservatives, and its national executive had a subcommittee for 'literature, research and publicity'. Central party organisations put out far more printed propaganda, which reached a peak in the 1920s. National party manifestos were issued at general elections and normally gave much more detail about policy than they had before the First World War. Conservative Central Office sold its candidates more than four leaflets for each voter at the 1929 election and used an advertising agency to improve its presentation.

National daily newspaper circulation grew from under 5½ million to nearly 10 million between 1920 and 1937. Radio first reached a mass audience in the 1920s and 1930s. Baldwin, as Conservative prime minister, used it effectively during the General Strike in 1926, and by the 1935 general election candidates were responding locally to what was said on national broadcasts.

Film was becoming important in politics for the first time. The public learnt about national and international issues from cinema newsreels, and the

Conservatives had the money to make their own films and send cinema vans round the country. By the 1931 election the party had 22 vans. Free film shows combining propaganda and entertainment could attract about 2,000 people a day in large towns.

Although local Liberal parties were often in disarray at the end of the First World War, both Conservatives and Labour built up their national organisations, expanding their women's sections and recruiting new members. Labour women's sections had representatives on the party's national executive and claimed approximately 300,000 members by 1929, though this apparently includes many who were affiliated through trade unions.

The job of agents and political parties was now changing. Less work was needed to get supporters on the electoral register as local councils saw to that. More work was needed to win over new voters and get them out at elections. Contests in each constituency were cheaper, but candidates were less likely to finance their own electioneering and national campaigns were becoming more complex and expensive, so constituency parties needed to mount a succession of fund-raising events.

Both parties employed more full-time agents after 1918, though the Conservative party advanced most with 352 agents who had passed professional examinations by 1937. Party membership seemed increasingly linked with class. Large numbers of working-class men and women must have voted Conservative, but local Conservative parties grew most in middle-class districts. Labour membership was lower, but the party gained support from large numbers of affiliated trade unionists.

The class divide was reflected in party MPs. The proportion of landowners declined on the Conservative side and around 40 per cent were businessmen in trade or industry between the First and Second World Wars. All except 8 of Labour's 57 MPs were sponsored by trade unions in 1918, though the parliamentary party gained a stronger middle-class membership after the 1922 election.

Local elections

Men and women got a parliamentary vote by simply living in a house, flat or room for six months, but they only had a vote in local council elections if they or their spouse were property owners or tenants who paid rates. The local council vote was available on much the same terms as before 1918, except that people were no longer disqualified because they received poor relief payments. In 1945 local council votes were given to all those able to vote in national elections.

Town council elections had often been based on party divisions in the nineteenth century, but the issues and loyalties were most frequently local. In the twentieth century they became more national. Labour candidates for local councils often linked their campaigns with the party's national policies, and in cities where they had a major impact council politics therefore became more closely associated with central government issues. Conservatives tended to resist this trend. Local Conservatives normally stood as independent candidates in country areas, whereas council elections in large towns were more likely to be fought on some sort of party lines. Local government was rather less democratic and partisan than Westminster politics before the Second World War.

Document case study

The debate in parliament on giving women equal voting rights with men in 1928

3.1 Sir W. Joynson-Hicks

The main opposition seems to me to be based on the ground that the control of political power will be transferred from men to women . . . that was the reason which moved the House in 1918, by a purely artificial restriction, to limit the number of women voters – in order that the objection . . . at that time to the political power passing from men to women should be artificially prevented. It was not then felt, I am sure, that women under 30 were any less fitted to exercise the franchise than men under 30. It was avowedly an experimental period . . .

Source: Hansard, 5th series, vol. 215, col. 1366–67

3.2 Sir G. Cockerill

I ask this question in all seriousness: whether women ought to be the determining factor in our political life? . . . Those who framed the last Act . . . gave women the vote at 30. They deliberately ignored individual equality; they secured approximately sex equality; they gave approximately equal power to men and women . . . They may have inflicted some injustice on individuals, and that is the injustice that this Bill is intended to remove, but they inflicted no injustice on the sexes, as this Bill, if uncorrected, most certainly will do . . . For my part, if either sex is to be supreme at the polls, I would prefer to see, quite frankly, men put in the supremacy.

Source: Hansard, 5th series, vol. 215, col. 1379–80

3.3 Colonel Applin

The wealth of this country, from which the revenues of the country are derived, is produced by men on the scale of 10:1. I have looked up the wills for last year, and I find that men left £58,000,000, whereas women left merely £6,000,000. That means that, if we are to have a majority rule by women in this country, we are handing over to them the taxable wealth of the country, to which they have contributed only one-tenth. [Laughter.] . . . We are governing a great Empire – and we forget it very often – and that Empire comprises not only our great self-governing Dominions, but the largest Mohammedan population in the world . . . Among the Mohammedans, women not only have no voice, but are not seen. What will be the effect on the great Mohammedan population of the world of granting the franchise in this country – the governing country

– to a majority of 2,200,000 women over men? [Laughter.] . . . In India, we have a terrible problem at this moment . . . what a weapon we will put into the hands of the agitators if we tell the Hindus of India that they are to be ruled by a majority of women!

Source: Hansard, 5th series, vol. 215, col. 1391

3.4 Countess of Iveagh

As regards the last extension of the franchise, in 1918 . . . it was granted, to a large extent, at any rate, in consequence of the part women had taken in the great national effort during the War, but, as a matter of fact, that Act was so adjusted as to exclude those women who had done most in industry to make up the great shortage of labour.

Source: Hansard, 5th series, vol. 215, col. 1393

3.5 Miss Wilkinson

There is a curious reluctance, especially in the Press, to admit the maturity of women . . . this proposal would not merely enfranchise a further number of women of a certain age, but it . . . would give the vote to a very important new class, and that is the whole class of independent women workers. It is frequently forgotten that a woman of the age of 30 or over does not get the vote under the present law unless she has either a husband or furniture.

Source: Hansard, 5th series, vol. 215, col. 1404

3.6 Mr Baldwin

To-night, we are asking this Parliament to fall in line with Australia, Canada, New Zealand and the United States of America, to mention only the English-speaking countries, in enfranchising men and women on the same basis . . . The minds and hearts of our people are fitted for the complete enfranchisement of women by the experience of the War . . . there was an overwhelming demonstration before our eyes of the part played by woman in every phase and sphere and function of our national life, and, to those of us who saw the part that she played in the War, there seems to be something almost ridiculous in refusing her claim to equal citizenship.

Source: Hansard, 5th series, vol. 215, col. 1407–08

Document case-study questions

1 In what ways do the documents suggest that the arrangements for women to have more restricted voting rights than men in 1918 were just and unjust?

2 (a) According to Documents 3.1 and 3.2, what are the dangers of giving all women the vote? (b) On what values and problems are these suggestions of danger based? (c) Why do you think the arguments in Document 3.3 were greeted by laughter in 1928? Compare the arguments with those in Document 2.2. To what extent do you think the views in Document 3.3 would have been taken more seriously before the First World War?

3 Why do these documents suggest that women were given the vote on equal terms with men in 1928 and not in 1918?

Notes and references

1 D. Tanner, *Political change and the Labour party 1900–1918*, Cambridge, 1990, p. 119.

4 Power in the state

The House of Commons had gradually come to be elected by more people, but how much power did it have? Government ministers gained greater control over party MPs in the House of Commons and introduced more laws. MPs gained more opportunities to check up on government ministers, and civil service power grew. Monarchs took less part in government after the death of Queen Victoria, and the House of Lords lost most of its power.

Historians and political scientists often think of those who run a country as doing three main jobs – what can be called the three main functions of government:

1 The legislative function – making laws.
2 The executive function – running or administering the country on a day-to-day basis. This includes defending the land by maintaining the armed forces and enforcing the laws by some kind of policing. As Chapters 5–7 show, the executive jobs expanded between 1830 and 1945 to include the provision of education and various kinds of welfare. In a complex industrial country the executive must also make policies for the long term.
3 The judicial function – judging those who might have broken criminal laws and punishing those who have, as well as dealing with civil disputes.

Broadly, the House of Commons together with the House of Lords had the legislative power. In theory the king or queen had executive powers, but in practice these were used by government ministers headed by the cabinet. They relied on a mass of *civil servants* to do the paperwork and ensure that the government could do what was necessary across the country as a whole.

The monarch

Monarchs traditionally appointed and dismissed prime ministers. William IV dismissed his Liberal prime minister, Lord Melbourne, in 1834, but his next minister, the Conservative leader Sir Robert Peel, soon failed to get majority support in the House of Commons at a general election and resigned. Monarchs did not dismiss their prime ministers any more after this. If a party with an overall majority in the House of Commons had a clear leader, the king or queen would have to appoint him as prime minister. But when there was no clear party leader or procedure for choosing one the monarch had to make the final decision. Queen Victoria (1837–1901) was able to choose Lord Rosebery as the new Liberal prime minister in 1894, and after consultation George V appointed Baldwin as Conservative prime minister in 1923. If no party had an overall majority in the Commons, again the monarch would have to use some judgement. George V played a key role in getting Ramsay MacDonald to continue as prime minister heading the coalition National government in 1931 when his Labour administration collapsed and no party had an overall Commons majority.

The appointment of cabinet ministers was largely a matter for the prime minister, but Queen Victoria had much influence. She kept Sir Charles Dilke out of Gladstone's cabinet in 1880 because he had been a republican, and insisted on Rosebery becoming the new foreign secretary in 1886. If there was a major disagreement between the two houses of parliament or a violent dispute between political groups within the nation, again the monarch might have a role. Queen Victoria mediated when there was disagreement between Lords and Commons after the Third Reform Act (p. 24), helping to bring the party leaders together. George V called a conference at Buckingham Palace in 1914 when conflict over Irish Home Rule looked likely to produce civil war.

The monarch, especially Queen Victoria, could still have a lot of influence in decision making. The famous constitutional writer Walter Bagehot described how the queen encouraged and warned her ministers. According to one historian[1] she used to instruct, abuse and hector her Liberal prime minister, Gladstone. She was in a particularly strong position to give advice on foreign policy in her later years. She greeted Lord Rosebery as her new foreign secretary in 1886 by explaining how she had 'nearly 50 years' experience, and has always watched particularly and personally over foreign affairs, and therefore knows them well'. In the end the queen did not have to be obeyed, but she could not be ignored. Ministers had to consult her about important church and state appointments. She devoted hours each day to reading and commenting on state papers, and in crises prime ministers might get up to six letters and telegrams a day from her. They had to reply. Historians do not quite know what overall effect this had, but Queen Victoria was certainly an active participant in state affairs, not just a ceremonial figurehead.

Later monarchs did not play the same role. Edward VII (1901–10) had more attractive things to do than spending hours reading state papers and writing notes and memos about them. The main political role of George V (1910–36) seems to have been that of trying to bring sides together in disputes, particularly Irish factions. George VI (1936–52) followed his father's model of kingship.

Government ministers

Prime ministers were appointed by monarchs, but it was clear long before 1830 that they needed support from a majority of MPs in the House of Commons to keep going. From 1868 a prime minister from one party would resign immediately after a general election if another party had an overall Commons majority – a clear acceptance that the electorate, not the king or queen, decided who was to govern. A prime minister who lost majority support would only stay and wait to see what happened in parliament if no other party or leader had an overall majority, as happened in 1885 and 1923. The prime minister or party leader and the ministers he appointed were there on a kind of mandate from the electorate. The powers they had came partly from the monarch and partly from parliament, and the House of Commons increasingly checked up on what they did.

The powers from the monarch were the royal prerogative powers. These were powers which monarchs had traditionally used to run the country from medieval times and which, at least in theory, had never been taken away from them. They included powers to manage foreign affairs, defence and public safety and included important rights to declare war and make treaties. By the mid-nineteenth century ministers largely held these powers. Parliament could enquire about them, criticise the way they were used and ultimately cut off the necessary money or force ministers to resign if it objected to what they did. Yet, as the powers were often not clearly defined in writing and much of what happened in government was secret, ministers had a lot of scope to act without public checks.

Other powers ministers held came from parliament. Laws were passed to deal with matters like poverty, public health and working conditions. Because the matters were complex, an increasing number of laws left ministers to decide the details of what should be done. Laws passed by parliament – so-called primary legislation – often gave ministers powers to draw up further regulations – secondary legislation. Many also allowed ministers and civil servants much freedom, or discretion, in deciding what should be done.

The cabinet

As today, the leading ministers were in the cabinet, which had grown in importance in the eighteenth and early nineteenth centuries. Collective cabinet responsibility – the understanding that all ministers must support all government policies or else resign – was developing rapidly in the 1830s. It was rare for ministers to vote against the government's line, even on minor matters, and every-thing ministers did was coming to be seen as part of a government's overall policy.

Although the cabinet was in charge of the executive, running the country on a day-to-day basis, it was very informal until the First World War. During the nineteenth century it would generally assemble once a week while parliament was sitting, but it would not have meetings from August to late October. A far more businesslike and managerial approach was required in the First World War, when formal cabinet minutes were taken for the first time. Meetings then involved not just agreements between top politicians but more administrative decisions and instructions for civil servants to carry out.

Government and parliament

Legislation

The cabinet relied on support in the House of Commons to continue in office. During the nineteenth century ministers, carrying out cabinet and government policy, also brought in more bills. In other words, the cabinet was taking up a part of the legislative (law-making) role as well as having an executive one administering the country.

Lord John Russell, the mid-nineteenth-century Liberal prime minister, described the change from the start of the century. He still saw ministers as 'chiefly appointed to administer the affairs of the Empire' – in other words, to act as an executive. But since 'the passing of the Reform Bill' in 1832 it had 'been thought convenient, on every subject on which an alteration of the law is required, that the government should undertake the responsibility of proposing it to parliament'. As law making became more complicated, it was often better for government lawyers rather than individual MPs to draw up bills. The MP's role was often to call on the government to bring in bills. The cabinet, which had developed as an executive, was beginning to produce a legislative programme. With a little exaggeration, the *Illustrated London News* suggested in 1861: 'All legislation is passing into the hands of the government.'

Government power in the House of Commons

To legislate, the government needed MPs' votes in the Commons and for these they relied on the party system and the whips who would encourage or instruct MPs to vote on party lines. The whips' influence increased considerably in the later nineteenth century. Discipline tightened particularly on the Conservative side in the 1880s and 1890s. Lord Salisbury, the leader, mentioned in 1889 how MPs were now 'all partisans', and the Conservative MP Arthur Griffith-Boscawen recalled feeling like a 'voting machine' in the 1890s.

This more partisan approach reflected how MPs were now elected more as representatives of national parties and leaderships. They relied on local election workers whose loyalties might be to the national party as much or more than to the constituency candidate (see p. 29). In these circumstances the parliamentary leaders were in a stronger position to get support. A growing number of divisions on government policy were seen as votes of confidence (ones which might bring the government down and possibly lead to a general election), and from the 1890s more MPs seem to have been looking for ministerial jobs, which did indeed multiply in the early twentieth century. How far then did the MPs whom voters actually chose still have power and freedom of action? Was the House of Commons, as some feared, becoming an assembly of men run by party machines?

In 1830 ministers and other MPs had virtually equal opportunity to bring in proposals for laws or motions for discussion, but by 1914 the government virtually controlled the parliamentary timetable. From the mid-1830s there was an understanding that government ministers' business should have priority on a couple of days in the week, and from the 1880s it had priority on well over 80 per cent of the days when the Commons sat.

Ministers were able to get new rules helping them control Commons business in the 1880s because Irish MPs were systematically disrupting parliament by filibustering – talking incessantly to waste other people's time and obstruct business. A procedure to close debates had to be introduced in 1882. A 'closure' vote could be taken if 40 MPs requested it, and a government with a Commons majority could easily get this. From 1887 ministers started using orders which limited the time to be spent discussing bills at different stages in the Commons – so-called guillotine motions. Introduced to deal with disruption from a small number of MPs, these were a wonderful way of helping governments get their bills through parliament. There were four guillotine motions in the ten years 1886–95, but they were used increasingly and there were ten in 1905–08. In 1902 Arthur Balfour as Conservative leader put together various rules which gave the government increased powers, a set of arrangements for controlling Commons time popularly known as the 'Parliamentary Railway Timetable'. (See the document case study for some of the debate on this.)

Commons scrutiny of the government

Government departments and agencies had to send regular reports to the House of Commons, and it was understood from the mid-nineteenth century that MPs could ask about anything a minister had or had not done in his job. Parliamentary question time developed. MPs asked ministers no questions in 1800. By 1850 there were only around 200 a year, but by the 1890s there were about 4,000 to 5,000, and many of these were followed by second or supplementary questions to get more details or score political points.

Parliament had a clear right to decide what taxes could be levied from the seventeenth century onwards. MPs could stop taxes and examine how the government spent its money but, unlike members of many foreign parliaments, from the mid-nineteenth century they have not been able to make the government tax or spend more. Rules introduced in 1852 and 1866 stated that only ministers could ask for money, but MPs did expand their ways of finding out how the money was spent, particularly by setting up the Public Accounts Committee in 1861.

The House of Lords

The House of Commons was thought to have sole control over tax and government spending, but the Lords had equal legislative power until 1911. Yet from the First Reform Act in 1832 it was clear that the Lords would have to give way to the Commons if there were a real struggle. Grey was then the only man the king could find who could govern as prime minister with majority support in the Commons. He eventually insisted that the king must promise to create the peers needed to get his reform bill through the Lords in 1832. Once the king had agreed, it was obvious that ultimately the elected House of Commons might insist on a major reform against the Lords' wishes. As its electorate grew, the Commons could claim a stronger mandate from the people, which the Lords would find it more difficult to oppose.

After the Second Reform Act, leading Conservative peers claimed that the Lords still had a part to play when government was based on the people's mandate. A House of Commons might pass a law which had not been clearly proposed by the leaders of the governing party at an election and which had therefore not been approved by the voters. Even if they had apparently approved a policy, the public might change their mind and need a second opportunity to vote on the issue. This meant that the Lords might reasonably reject a bill supported by the Commons and insist that they would not agree to it without a general election. This argument was all the stronger when guillotine procedures were used in the Commons and a government might push measures through without proper discussion by the people's representatives. The Lords seemed to carry out their role effectively when they rejected the Gladstone government's Second Irish Home Rule Bill after its approval by the Commons in 1893. They turned the bill down by a 10–1 margin, and the Conservatives who campaigned against it won a large majority over the Liberals at the following general election in 1895.

There were, however, two key problems with the Lords' view. As an obviously wealthy and privileged minority – '500 men . . . chosen accidentally from among the unemployed', as the Liberal minister Lloyd George put it – they seemed a strange group to judge and act on the will of the people. Secondly, after Liberal splits in 1886, the Conservative or Unionist party opposing Irish Home Rule was dominant in the Lords. The house looked too much like an unelected but powerful branch of the Conservative party – the Conservative leader's 'poodle' rather than 'the watchdog of the constitution', as Lloyd George put it.

When the Lords rejected the Liberal 'people's budget' in 1909, they were going against a custom dating from the seventeenth century that they did not alter Commons decisions about money. The Lords were consistent in following their theory about the people's mandate. When there was a Commons majority for the budget again after the January 1910 election, they duly passed it, but the Liberal prime minister, Herbert Asquith, was then able to end the Lords' right to stop new laws. After the 1911 Parliament Act they could only delay measures passed by the Commons for two years.

Peers often remained as important ministers. Foreign secretaries were in the Lords from 1868 to 1905 continuously, and about a third of major cabinet ministers were there before the First World War. Seven of the 16 members of Bonar Law's cabinet were in the Lords in 1922, but when Bonar Law retired in 1923, Conservative leaders decided that he could not be replaced by Lord Curzon because he was a peer. George V had to make the final decision, and later gave this explanation to Curzon. It reflected the dominance of the House of Commons over the Lords, but there was a further reason: the Labour party, which was now the main opposition, was scarcely represented among the peers. By the First World War Britain, unlike most other advanced industrial countries, had only one assembly which had significant power in making laws. The Liberals' Parliament Act suggested that the Lords would be reformed 'on a popular instead of hereditary basis'. After the First World War many Conservatives argued for some reform, so that there would be a powerful second chamber which could effectively alter or revise legislation. At the end of the twentieth century, it has not yet come.

The civil service

In the early nineteenth century ministers could run departments themselves, making all the important decisions while their secretaries in the civil service just did the writing. In the period 1830–1945 government departments had far more to do (see Chapters 5–7). At the same time ministers had to spend longer dealing with parliament, responding to MPs' questions and getting approval for complex legislation. This provided new opportunities for civil servants to gain power.

Ministers increasingly depended on them for advice about policy. With more complex laws to administer and services to provide, some decisions inevitably had to be left to civil servants. Ministers made political calculations, decided general lines of policy and presented them to parliament and the public. They looked to civil servants for many of the ideas and most of the details. Sir Robert Morant, the permanent secretary at the Board of Education, for example, was largely responsible for the details of the 1902 Education Act and the introduction of school medical inspections in 1907. Ministers defended what civil servants did; civil servants might ensure ministers did not make administrative mistakes. The civil service machine and its power expanded in other advanced countries like Germany, France and the USA. Politicians needed its support, and its development was inevitable when the state's functions grew, but the result was shifts in power much less open to public view than those between the executive and other MPs.

This increased influence also made civil service efficiency more important. Examinations were gradually introduced in different departments from 1870. Fewer civil servants were promoted through *patronage* – from their connections with important people – and more through showing academic merit. The civil service thus became more meritocratic. The early examinations for top civil servants were linked with courses at Oxford and Cambridge which few outside the wealthy classes could enter, so there was no real equality in line with democratic ideas. This came only with more scholarships in the twentieth century (see pp. 78 and 99).

The Treasury

Within government the Treasury had the massive power which came from controlling the money – a power which politicians and reformers who wanted to spend a lot often found very frustrating. The chancellor of the exchequer, Sir Charles Wood, referred to the extra work the Treasury had to do exercising a 'more rigorous control over the expenditure of all other departments' in 1850. The prime minister, Lord Salisbury, commented in 1899 that 'because every policy at every step required money the Treasury can veto everything'.

After the First World War the Treasury's control was consolidated. Its top official, the permanent secretary, became head of the civil service as a whole, and a department in the Treasury was in charge of running it. Rules in 1920 and 1924 ensured that no proposals which involved spending money could be debated in cabinet before they had been discussed with the Treasury. Many historians and politicians have seen the government's limited or traditional economic and social policies between the First and Second World Wars as a result of Treasury power.

Conclusion

The roles of the Commons, Lords and cabinet were largely transformed between 1830 and 1914. By the First World War something like the modern balance of power and functions was established. Yet the balance was always evolving and changing. Prime ministerial power has fluctuated greatly in the twentieth century; almost unmentioned in law, it has apparently varied markedly with the holder of the office. Lloyd George increased it during the First World War, but it diminished to some extent in the 1920s after public disapproval of his methods. Civil servants did much more and seemed to have more power up to 1945, but this again depended on relationships between ministers and officials, which were perpetually changing out of the public view. Some of the shifts in power can be charted in laws and political commentaries; many depend on subtle changes in personal relationships. The next three chapters examine how the state's powers increased and what effect that had on ordinary people's lives.

Document case study

Government control in the House of Commons in the early twentieth century

4.1 The leader of the opposition's view of opportunities for MPs

Sir Henry Campbell-Bannerman, 1902

there is the right of private Members who have introduced Bills of their own, or who wish to bring before the House Motions [propositions for debate] of their own. I admit, for my part, that that is not now so important a function of the private Member [an individual MP outside the government] as it was some twenty or thirty or forty years ago . . . I admit also that such is the pressure of business in the House that the private Members have less and less chances of effective legislation; and the power to legislate falls more and more into the hands of the Government of the day. I admit all this, but there is something quite apart from this right of the private Member to move and to introduce a Bill on his own account; there is the general right of the House to interrogate Ministers and discuss questions, and to inform the opinion of the country by so doing . . . And it is this, I think, which is the most important thing to bear in mind when we speak of the rights of the House and the rights of private Members.

Source: Hansard, 4th series, vol. 102, quoted in V. Cromwell, *Revolution or evolution: British government in the nineteenth century*, London, 1977, pp. 178–79

4.2 A government minister's view

Joseph Chamberlain, 1902

I believe that the people who elect the majority of the House have a right to see that that majority has power to carry out what is . . . the will of the majority of the nation; and our elections and our representative system are a perfect and absolute farce if with one hand you pretend that the majority elects a Government, and then with the other hand prevent that Government from doing its proper work . . .

Source: Hansard, 4th series, vol. 102, quoted in Cromwell, *Revolution or evolution*, p. 181

4.3 The view of a Liberal MP and historian

James Bryce, 1902

When I entered Parliament in 1880 many of the best and most useful Bills passed by the House, were introduced by private Members. They were not Bills which excited political conflict, out of which party capital could be made, but they dealt with comparatively small defects in the law, which the Government did not care to deal with, but of which the private Member happened to know, and thus they were remedied. In those days a private Member could hope to carry his Bill; there were opportunities of doing so . . . It is a great loss to the country that private Members can no longer pass such Bills . . .

Source: Hansard, 4th series, vol. 102, quoted in Cromwell, *Revolution or evolution*, pp. 183–84

4.4 A constitutional writer's description

J. Redlich, 1908

when the division bell rings he [an MP] hurries to the House, and is told by his whip whether he is an 'aye' or a 'no'. Sometimes he is told that party tellers have not been put on, and that he can vote as he pleases. But open questions are not popular; they compel a member to think for himself, which is always troublesome. Not that a member is a mere pawn in the game, but the number of questions which even a member of Parliament has leisure and capacity to think out for himself is necessarily limited.

Source: J. Redlich, *The procedure of the House of Commons*, London, 1908, quoted in G. W. Cox, *The efficient secret: the cabinet and the development of political parties in Victorian England*, Cambridge, 1987, p. 66

4.5 Newspaper comment

The Times, *1909*

With a large and faithful majority behind them, Ministers may stifle debate at their pleasure. They can refuse to allow their opponents to develop inconvenient arguments . . . by resort to the ordinary closure . . . By a deft arrangement of clauses and of hours they can shut out discussion altogether on the most essential provisions of their Bills . . .

Source: *The Times*, 2 September 1909, quoted in Jane Ridley, *The Unionist opposition and the House of Lords, 1906–10, Parliamentary history*, vol. 11, p. 239

Document case-study questions

1 What is the argument in Document 4.3 in favour of private members' legislation?

2 What are the most important rights which, according to Document 4.1, individual MPs have, apart from introducing laws?

3 (a) What is the argument in Document 4.2 in favour of ministerial power in the House of Commons? (b) With reference to Documents 4.4 and 4.5, and drawing on what you know of the electoral system and the government's functions, how strong do you think the case in Document 4.2 is?

4 How important and useful do these documents suggest the role of an individual MP was in the first decade of the twentieth century?

Notes and references

1 H. C. G. Matthew, *Gladstone 1874–98*, p. 260.

5 The role of the state, 1830–1867 – an age of laissez faire?

The 1830–70 period is often described as an age of laissez faire. Thinkers who believed that the government should play only a small part in economic and social life had some influence, but there is much debate about how great this was. Although there was a major move towards free trade, the government was more active in a wide range of ways.

The state in 1830

The state means different things to different people – an area of land, the use of power or a set of rights and regulations. Let's say it is the organisation which has supreme power over certain territory. It includes not only what we call central government but also the apparatus the government uses to keep power – the army, law courts and the employees we know as civil servants or bureaucrats. In the early 1830s ordinary citizens did not see many signs of all this – just a few tax collectors and Post Office officials and occasionally some soldiers. Britain had about 21,000 *civil servants* for around 16 million people compared with around half a million for a population of 56 million in the 1990s, and most of them were involved in tax collecting. The central government departments dealing with overseas matters had 106 employees and those running domestic affairs only 101.

Laissez-faire ideas

Obviously the state did much less than it attempts now. This, it is said, was the great age of laissez faire, which translates roughly as the government letting citizens get on with their own business. Historians have distinguished between the individualism of the 1830–70 period and the *collectivism* which developed in the late nineteenth and twentieth centuries, when the state regulated and acted more for the community as a whole. There has been much debate among scholars about whether there was ever a true age of laissez faire and whether making a distinction between individualism and collectivism really helps in understanding the nature of government.

The starting point for this debate is the work of the late eighteenth- and early nineteenth-century writers known as 'classical economists'. The most important was the Scotsman Adam Smith, whose thinking guided and inspired the others. Smith believed in what we call a *free market economy*, where people buy and exchange goods among themselves without restriction and employers and workers bargain over pay and working conditions without government regulation. He thought businessmen who set out to make a profit for themselves also helped others by providing cheaper goods and more jobs, and that the state should let this beneficial process continue.

Smith said the government had three duties: 'first, the duty of protecting the society from the violence and invasion of other individual societies; secondly, the duty of protecting, as far as possible, every member of the society from the injustice or oppression of every member of it, or the duty of establishing an exact administration of justice; and, thirdly, the duty of erecting and maintaining certain public works and . . . institutions', which would not be profitable for individuals but helped society.

The first duty is what we call defence. The second is maintaining law and order, which any state has to do to keep power; but what sort of community services does the third suggest? Thinkers who followed Smith wanted economic freedom and low taxes, but even Nassau Senior, one of the more extreme laissez-faire enthusiasts, wrote of the government doing whatever helped 'the welfare of the governed'.

Bentham and the utilitarians

These ideas were developed much further by Jeremy Bentham, who was probably the most influential political thinker of the time. He saw the government's job as working for the greatest happiness of the greatest number of people. He thought this could be calculated, and that if enough information were gathered the correct way might be found to achieve maximum happiness. Bentham and his followers – utilitarians, as they were known – thus saw an important role for central government in enquiring into problems and carrying out uniform solutions. Yet he also believed in Adam Smith's ideas about leaving individuals alone as much as possible to achieve happiness in their own way in a free market economy. Only when one person's way of achieving happiness upset another's should the state intervene. Bentham saw government action as a necessary 'evil', and Adam Smith thought there should be a 'presumption' against it. The state, then, might have plenty to do, but the need for it to do anything had to be proved.

How important were political and economic theorists?

The main political thinkers and economists struck a balance rather than being either rigid opponents of state action or enthusiasts for it. Bentham in particular suggested a method of dealing with problems rather than a set of clear solutions, but how far did these theorists actually alter what happened? Again, historians disagree.

Important thinkers often influence us without our knowing it. Today we often interpret what people do in terms of sex or think that the government should act to reduce unemployment. These ideas stem to a considerable extent from the findings of the psychologist Sigmund Freud and the economist John Maynard Keynes in the early twentieth century. It is not that we have generally read either Freud or Keynes, but that their ideas have been popularised by a host of authors, journalists and television commentators and have become part of everyday thinking. Smith, Bentham and the other classical economists and utilitarians may have been difficult to read, but plenty of authors and journalists used their ideas, many of which came through in politicians' writings and speeches.

In Bentham's case the connections between thinker and government action are unusually clear. He advocated systematic inquiries and royal commissions to make these were used as never before: over a hundred were established between 1832 and 1850. He thought that well-trained men in central government needed to apply uniform solutions, and a mass of inspectors was set up to do this from 1828. By 1856 there were 16 sets of them, including ones for the poor law, public health, prisons, mines and schools. It may be hard to prove that commissions or inspectors were actually set up because of Bentham's writings, but the influence of his secretary, Edwin Chadwick, was unquestionable. Although Chadwick did not agree with all his employer's ideas, Bentham was, as his daughter put it, his 'guiding star'. Chadwick wrote the report of a royal commission on textile factories leading to a factory act in 1833, and the recommendations of the poor law commissioners which resulted in a great reform in 1834, and he produced a report on sanitary conditions in 1842 which led to changes under the 1848 Public Health Act. He was secretary to the poor law commissioners established in 1834 to administer the new poor law and a commissioner on the General Board of Health set up in 1848.

Whereas some historians have seen reforms as a product of ideology, others view them as practical answers to practical problems. Back in the 1950s and 1960s Oliver MacDonagh argued that the government acted because people were suffering 'intolerable' hardships and reform came piecemeal as campaigners and government inspectors revealed more and more 'intolerable' things.[1]

There are, of course, many valid ways of explaining reforms. The 1833 Factory Act can be seen as a compromise between campaigners outraged at child suffering in textile mills and employers who said they needed cheap labour to remain competitive. It was also largely based on a scheme worked out by Chadwick using Bentham's methods.

Similarly, parts of the 1834 Poor Law Amendment Act were based on Bentham's writings about how poor people who did not support themselves must have a less 'eligible' (desirable) life than those who made their own living. Yet recent historians have explained the new policy as being as much a result of landowners' anxiety to reduce local taxes to support the poor as of a belief in Bentham's ideas or a free labour market. Some of these landowners were influenced by the classical economists' ideas, but there has been lively historical controversy about how extensive this influence was.[2]

It is often unrealistic to distinguish between using theory and finding practical solutions. As circumstances change, so thinkers like Smith, Bentham and Nassau Senior produce theories to deal with them. On the other hand, businessmen and politicians take up the theories that meet their needs or serve their own self-interest, and people decide what is intolerable according to fashionable ideas of right and wrong. How far can historians really distinguish between self-interested, practical, theoretical and idealistic motives?

Local government

It should be easier to work out what was done than why people did it. The main problem here is that the ministers and civil servants in the central government did not administer very much around the country. They relied on local authorities to carry out their instructions. The state decided what powers these should have, and a growing number of statutes – laws passed by parliament – stated what local authorities must, could and could not do, but it was still hard to control them.

The core of England's local government system in 1830 dated from medieval and Tudor times. *Justices of the Peace* (JPs) – generally wealthy local landowners who were not paid for their work – supervised a range of local services like helping the poor and maintaining roads, but the services themselves were largely provided within each parish. Parishes are the area served by a parish church and vary vastly in size. Unpaid or poorly paid parish officers – like overseers of the poor, parish surveyors of highways, constables and nightwatchmen – applied laws after a fashion, and vestries (meetings of householders) could decide to take extra initiatives. Some, particularly in towns, set about providing what we consider normal public services such as paving, lighting, water supply and sewerage, but many did not.

Older towns often had their own corporations, but these were bodies which looked after their own property, ate dinners and elected MPs, rather than acting in the public interest like modern town councils. Separate groups of improvement commissioners were often set up to provide basic services. When the Whig government replaced the old corporations by elected ones in 1835, they thought of them as groups to represent middle-class opinion and keep order rather than as administrators to provide basic services like street cleaning and sewers. The new corporations had the power to do these things if they wanted, and they could take over from existing improvement commissioners, but they were not expected to do so. As time went on, larger towns set up their own corporations. Some started ambitious schemes of civic improvement, and statute laws gave them new responsibilities.

Unfortunately, new responsibilities and improvements meant new local taxes. Central government directives which involved spending money were often unpopular. What actually happened was not so much what the state ordered as the outcome of a many-sided conflict between central government, local officials and different groups of ratepayers who chose local authorities and fought elections with enthusiasm and ill feeling.

The role of the state

Defence

What then was the state able to do? Its first duty was defence. It had a tax-collecting system which employed most of its civil servants, and in the early 1830s it spent £40 million of its £53 million annual income on the armed forces and paying interest on the National Debt, which had been run up to pay for past wars.

Law and order

Its next concern was law and order, but this was largely left to local authorities; the Home Office, the central government department responsible, had a staff of 32 officials in 1832. The home secretary had one police force under his command – London's Metropolitan Police, established in 1829 – and he could use these in other areas if he wished, as, for example, during Chartist disturbances in 1839. The main job specified for the new municipal corporations in 1835 was to look after policing; a law in 1839 allowed JPs to use county police forces and another in 1856 compelled them to do so. For many townspeople the new police must have been the most obvious sign of growing state power. *Working-* and *middle-class* people often welcomed them as a safeguard against crime, but they also set about removing some of the old unruly street life. They were one reason for the disappearance of the street theatre politics described in Chapter 1. They enabled Manchester Council, for example, to clear away many street sellers and stop cruel sports in the 1830s and 1840s, and the late nineteenth-century *socialist* William Morris claimed that they made the streets 'decent prison corridors, with people just trudging to and from their work'.

National government had a loose control over prisons until it took them over in 1877. Earlier, JPs supervised them with visits from central government inspectors after 1835. The nineteenth-century equivalent of borstals – reformatory schools for youths under 16 – were run by voluntary groups with the state providing money and sending inspectors.

The poor law

The state had laws to help the poor from Tudor times – JPs and parish overseers of the poor carried them out and had a lot of freedom in deciding how help should be given. The 1834 Poor Law Amendment Act introduced the first set of civil servants to administer the poor law on a national basis, and they were to introduce a new system under which fit and able-bodied people could get help only in harshly run workhouses. Nevertheless, guardians of the poor elected by ratepayers were to run the system at a local level, and the civil servants – the poor law commissioners and their assistants – had limited powers. They could control the appointment, dismissal and conditions of employees, but they could not order the guardians to build the workhouses on which the new system depended. This was the first attempt to get local authorities to introduce reforms under detailed government supervision; the commissioners in London sent out regulations and instructions about how to treat *paupers*, and assistant commissioners travelled the country to supervise and cajole. Local research has revealed a mixed response. Many guardians co-operated with the poor law commissioners, and assistant commissioners got a lot done, but they had a hard time, especially in the industrial north. Guardians meeting at Huddersfield in 1837 had to escape through the back door of their workhouse while a crowd of thousands threw stones at the front.

Large numbers of fit and healthy people continued to get help in their own homes. The overseers and officials who had run the old system frequently ran the new one. It was difficult to get poorly paid officers to meet new standards of efficiency, and often little changed. For example, when the guardians of the Chelmsford Union in Essex were looking around for a master to be in charge of their new workhouse, they could find no one better than the man who ran their old one. After several problems over the way he managed work for his own profit, they eventually dismissed him for being in the pub, having left his workhouse unsupervised at a time when keeping discipline was difficult. The new poor law was an ambitious attempt to gain more uniformity and efficiency across England and Wales, and it worked falteringly. In Scotland the government was less ambitious. Instead of introducing the same workhouse scheme, in 1845 they set up the Board of Supervision which would oversee parish officers and had less centralising powers than the English commissioners.

Religion and morality

The state had traditionally undertaken another duty which most nineteenth-century politicians thought vital – maintaining morality and religion. This included using a licensing system to regulate the sale of alcohol in the interests of morality and public order. Most importantly, it involved supporting the Church of England, similar *Anglican* churches in Wales and Ireland and the rather different Church of Scotland. These were established churches, which meant that they had rights to levy taxes like tithes and church rates, kept large estates and were regulated by law. They taught standards of right and wrong and preached religious truth, providing the morality which Conservatives and many Liberal politicians thought vital to any proper Christian state.

Education

From the 1830s the government took up one new responsibility which most nineteenth-century people connected with security and religion – supporting education. As the Whig MP and historian Lord Macaulay put it, 'if you take away education, what means do you leave' to protect persons and property? 'You leave means which only necessity can justify . . . You leave guns and bayonets, stocks and whipping post, treadmills, solitary cells, penal colonies and gibbets.' Better perhaps to give a little help to the schools already set up by religious societies. Money was first given for building schools and later for equipment, teacher training and normal running costs. As the state gave funds, it wanted to supervise how the money was spent, and a system of school inspectors developed from 1839. With grants increasing from £20,000 in 1833 to £724,000 in 1860, the government needed to check on achievement. From 1862 the money was therefore given according to the results of examinations which school inspectors carried out. The state did not yet run its own schools, but its inspectors gained real power when school finance and teachers' salaries depended on their judgements.

Factory regulation

Apart from education, the state took on new jobs that became necessary because of population growth, industrialisation and town expansion – in short, to deal with the effects of the Industrial Revolution. The need for this is obvious, whether the action is seen as a response to utilitarian thinking or to horror at 'intolerable' evils. For instance, the government needed population figures both to make utilitarian calculations and to find out the age of exploited children, so the registration of births, deaths and marriages was introduced to provide statistics for England and Wales in 1837 and for Scotland from 1855.

Working long hours in factories was very different from working them at home or even in village workshops. A series of laws introduced safety regulations for textile mills and restricted children's working hours there from 1833; women's hours were controlled from 1844. From 1842 the law also prevented women and boys under 10 from working underground in coal mines. Government inspectors checked that employers were obeying the law, but there has been disagreement about their effectiveness. Local *magistrates*, who judged cases brought in court, were often factory or mine owners themselves but, on the other hand, inspectors were frequently successful in getting offenders fined. Whatever their effect, up to the 1860s the law only controlled hours and working conditions in textile mills and coal mines. The limits on the working day were extended to factories as a whole in 1867, and it was left to local authorities to decide whether to enforce the restrictions in workshops with under 50 people. Of course, the restrictions were only for women and children. There was no direct regulation of any men's hours until the end of the nineteenth century.

Public health

Rapidly expanding towns produced new health problems. Early initiatives to provide sewers and piped water were taken by citizens and businessmen who set up improvement commissioners. Although dungheaps created a public health problem, sewage disposal was treated as a private matter. Householders paid for connections with the sewers, and those who had made their own arrangements did not see why they should later pay for other people's as well. Commissioners provided a service, but did not feel they had a public duty to extend it. Many town corporations gained their own laws to extend services like sewers, water pipes and street lighting from the 1840s, but there were great disputes about the cost. Householders did not like paying local taxes to fund new schemes. The 1848 Public Health Act set up the General Board of Health and outlined arrangements for local boards of health to provide combined water supply and sewerage schemes. However, the General Board of Health had little power to give orders and, unless an area had an unusually high death rate, it was up to local citizens and town corporations whether they had a local board in the first place. The state had little power; the General Board became unpopular and was wound up in 1858. The Privy Council's medical department took over what responsibility central government had for public health, but it had few powers. The home secretary gained authority to force local health boards to improve sewerage in 1866, but the state had not yet established a uniform system for improving public health.

Medical care and other services

There was more decisive action over individual medical care. Poor law guardians had to provide free vaccination against smallpox under a law of 1840, and this vaccination became compulsory in 1853. However harsh the regime for fit people was, local poor law boards generally gave poor families free medical treatment in their own homes, and from the 1850s many opened dispensaries to distribute medicines. Although the state did not think of providing general hospitals, the poor law authorities provided more beds for sick people and often built their own hospitals, apart from workhouses. By 1861 50,000 of the 65,000 hospital beds in England and Wales were provided by poor law unions.

Victorian parliaments had some rather more imaginative ideas about what local councils might do. They could, if they wished, provide extra services under the 1846 Baths and Washhouses Act or the 1855 Libraries Act, but while they could erect libraries, they could not build ordinary homes. Housing was seen as a private and commercial affair, not a public service.

Economic regulation

The state was obviously doing more to regulate the way people lived together; in other words, it was bringing in social reform. At the same time, it removed many controls on the way people gained their wealth – what we call economic affairs. In past centuries the state had regulated wages, prices and working hours and controlled who could do certain jobs through *apprenticeship laws*. This had largely stopped well before 1830, and laws controlling these things were often scrapped in the early nineteenth century, when they were no longer applied anyway.

Taxation

In 1830 the government still levied numerous taxes on imports and had restrictions on which foreign ships could transport goods to Britain. Some of the taxes were designed to ensure that people bought home-produced goods rather than foreign ones, which were made expensive by these import duties. A few were designed to ensure that goods came from one foreign region rather than another and therefore helped the economy of particular British colonies. All these taxes and restrictions disappeared over the next 30 years. In the mid-nineteenth century Britain became a 'free trade' country. Some quite heavy taxes were still levied on imports, but they were designed to get income for the government, not to restrict trade or encourage people to buy British goods. In this way trade was 'free', and historians sometimes see economic laissez faire contrasting with increased social regulation.

How much did the state regulate the economy?

In fact, however much freedom was possible in overseas trade, social needs led to regulation of economic affairs at home. Factory acts, for example, altered manufacturers' costs by limiting child labour. Economists and politicians both saw that the state sometimes had to act so that the community as a whole benefited from the goods and services in a growing economy.

The classical economists showed that the free market benefited all when there was competition between traders to sell their goods or services. If a trader faced no effective competition from other suppliers, and so had a monopoly, the situation was very different. This was a problem with railway companies when there was normally only one line between two towns and it would have made no sense to build two lines to compete for the same traffic. Here there was an inevitable monopoly, and classical economists readily saw the need for intervention. Politicians acted very soon after the first railway boom, establishing a railway department at the Board of Trade in 1842, with new safety regulations and inspectors to supervise them. An act in 1844 included powers to control railway companies' profits and charges and forced companies to run at least one cheap passenger train each day if they provided any passenger services.

Railway price controls and safety regulations are only two examples of government protection for consumers. Laws regulated conditions on passenger ships taking emigrants out of the country. There was a whole series of statutes about the sale of goods; basic items like coal and bread had to be sold by weight under acts from 1835 and 1836, and there were several new laws about the weights and measures to be used and how items were to be marked. The 1860 Adulteration of Food and Drink Act gave local authorities power to appoint food analysts and prosecute traders who were selling bad food. Consumer protection laws might seem very inadequate by today's standards, but this was partly because of inexperience in working out the necessary regulations and limited scientific knowledge. It was generally accepted that when consumers could not judge something adequately, they needed legal safeguards.

Was there an age of laissez faire?

While it gave up the regulation of overseas trade then, the state intervened to protect people when they worked, travelled or went shopping. Government inspectors were almost unknown in 1830; by 1867 they examined railways, ships, mines, factories, prisons, schools, workhouses and dungheaps. Whether there were enough of them and whether they had enough power to do their job properly are doubtful. State control grew unevenly and irregularly; it expanded rapidly in the 1830s, falteringly in the 1840s and variably in the 1850s. State action went much further in Ireland, including government transport and land improvement schemes to help poorer areas. In Britain central government still relied on local authorities to provide most services. A range of different local boards was set up as the government discovered new jobs to be done, and new tasks were given to authorities established for a completely different purpose. By 1867 poor law guardians in the countryside were often supervising sewers, rural police and the local election register. It all seemed rather chaotic, and there were important gaps.

Moreover, the British government did less than many of its European counterparts. The Prussian government was running a state education system in northern Germany while Britain sent inspectors round a haphazardly distributed assortment of schools set up by private charities. One eminent historian, Colin Matthew, suggests 'no industrial society can ever have existed in which the state played a smaller role than that of the United Kingdom in the 1860s'. Does this mean it was an age of laissez faire, or was it just a time when the government responded differently to different social and economic needs?

Document case study

Laissez faire and the debate over restricting children's working hours in textile factories

5.1. Adam Smith outlines the second duty of the state

The wealth of nations, *1776*

the duty of protecting, as far as possible, every member of the society from the injustice or oppression of every other member of it, or the duty of establishing an exact administration of justice . . .

Source: D. Fraser, *The evolution of the British welfare state*, 1st edn, London, 1973, p. 246

5.2 *The Economist* outlines the dangers of state action

The Economist, *21 November 1846*

the general helplessness of the masses . . . is sure to be induced by the state undertaking to provide for their welfare . . . while there is a great chance of individuals providing for their own welfare as individuals, there is almost an infinity of chances against their promoting the welfare of the community, when they attempt to do that by commercial and economical legislation.

Source: E. J. Evans (ed.), *Social policy 1830–1914: individualism, collectivism and the origins of the welfare state*, London, 1978, p. 29

5.3 The case for protecting factory children

Lord Macaulay, a Liberal MP and historian, in the House of Commons, 22 May 1846

I am as firmly attached as any Gentleman in the House to the principle of free trade properly stated, and I should state that principle in these terms: that it is not desirable the State should interfere with the contracts of persons of ripe age and sound mind, touching matters purely commercial . . . but you would fall into error if you apply it to transactions which are not purely commercial. Is there a single Gentleman so zealous for the principle of free trade as not to admit that he might consent to the restriction of commercial transaction when higher and other considerations are concerned?

. . . where the health of the community is concerned, the principle of non-interference does not apply without very great restrictions.

. . . the great mass of the people should not live in a way the effect of which is to abridge life, to make it wretched and feeble while it lasts, and to send to untimely graves the population . . . if it be the fact that places calculated to shorten life, to taint the health and to turn the stomach of those accustomed to more cleanly habits, are noxious to those who dwell in them; this proves how greatly the government of this country has neglected its duty, and proves that they have tolerated the existence of houses like hogstyes, until there is a danger of the population becoming like hogs. Who can affirm, then, with respect to a question where morality and humanity are concerned, that we must adhere to this principle of non-interference?

. . . is not the public health concerned in a question relating to the time of labour? Does any one who has examined the evidence, or opened his eyes in the world, or examined his own feelings, doubt that twelve hours a day of factory labour are more than are desirable for youths of thirteen? . . . Can any one doubt . . . that education is a matter of the highest importance, as regards the virtue and happiness of the common people? . . . Do we believe that, after twelve hours have been taken from the day for factory labour, and after so much time as is necessary for refreshment and exercise . . . that enough time will remain for that amount of education which it is desirable that people should have? . . . Now, I ask, whether it is not a rule universally adopted by all civilized society . . . that those who are of tender age should be placed under the guardianship of the State? No one would say that a rich person under age should be permitted to sign away his property . . . a boy of immature age cannot secure himself from injury, and the State is his guardian. But the property of the poor and young lies in his health and strength and skill – in the health both of his body and of his mind . . .

Source: Hansard, 3rd series, vol. 86, col. 1031–35

5.4 The problems with state protection

Sir Robert Peel, the former prime minister, replies

with regard to adult labour employed in the cotton, linen, woollen, and silk factories, you are about to impose what is equivalent to an income tax of 15 per cent on the labour of the adult. You are going to tell him, 'You shan't have the opportunity of labouring for more than ten hours, whereas you have hitherto been obliged to labour twelve hours': and do you believe, if you really establish that restriction – do you concur with the right hon. Gentleman in the belief that, for ten hours' labour, the operative can receive twelve hours' pay?

Source: Hansard, 3rd series, vol. 86, col. 1064–65

Document case-study questions

1 Does the description of the second duty of the state in Document 5.1 suggest that the government should restrict children's working hours?

2 What reasons does Document 5.3 give for the state to limit children's working hours in factories?

3 What arguments do Documents 5.2 and 5.4 give against restriction? How could the claims in Document 5.4 be used to illustrate the argument in Document 5.2?

4 How far are the arguments in these documents (a) moral (concerned with principles of right and wrong), (b) social (about how people live together), or (c) economic (about creating wealth)?

Notes and references

1 O. MacDonagh, *Early Victorian government, 1830–1870*, London, 1977.

2 A. Brundage, *The making of the new poor law 1832–39*, London, 1978; P. Mandler, *Aristocratic government in the age of reform*, Oxford, 1990. For a summary of the controversy see A. Brundage, D. Eastwood and P. Mandler, 'The making of the new poor law redivivus', *Past and Present*, no. 127, 1990.

6 The interventionist state, 1867–1914

New thinking led the government to do far more in 1867–1914 than in the earlier period. The types of regulation introduced in 1830–67 were extended. The government was more involved in employer–worker relations and welfare measures, but in many ways Britain remained a free market economy.

Historians generally see a change in the role of the state – often described as a shift from individualism to *collectivism* – soon after 1867, around the 1870s and 1880s. In other words, instead of every state action needing careful justification as some sort of necessary evil, people thought more of a government's duty to improve life for the community. Governments did more things, employed more people, spent more money and thought more about the need for action rather than the dangers of interference. They still believed in a *free market economy* and keeping state spending down, but more regulation and more taxpayers' money gradually seemed necessary to deal with national problems.

Growth in the state

Existing government departments expanded, and new ones like the Boards of Agriculture and Education were created in 1894 and 1899. The number of civil servants (government employees) grew from 54,000 in 1871 to 116,000 in 1901 and 282,000 in 1914. Central and local government had generally taken a declining proportion of gross national product (GNP, the total national wealth produced each year) in the mid-nineteenth century; it fluctuated from year to year and went up markedly if the government became involved in war, but overall it seems to have fallen from about 15 per cent to 9 per cent between 1830 and 1870. Then the state spent about the same share of GNP until the 1890s, when it took a rising proportion, though this does not seem to have gone far above 10 per cent before 1914. This compares with 50 per cent in the 1960s and well over 40 per cent in the 1990s. Yet with rising wealth the government was still able to spend far more. It is estimated that central and local government spending went up about ten times from 1870 to 1914, and that was in a period when prices overall had gone down. Central government taxes, which took an average of £1.89 per person in the population in the year 1870, amounted to £3.43 per person in the years just before the First World War,[1] and local government became more active and costly as well.

Reasons for state intervention

Empire

Why did the state have to do far more in 1914 than it had done in 1867? Part of the answer lay overseas; this was the main period of European empire building. By 1914 Britain controlled a quarter of the earth's land surface. In size and population it had the greatest empire the world had ever known, but Britain had rivals and its colonies needed defending. Concerns about naval strength forced governments to spend more on shipbuilding, and the army was a worry as well. In 1899–1902 Britain fought the Second Boer War against two South African republics occupied by about half a million men, women and children descended from former Dutch and French settlers. It should have been a walkover for the greatest empire on earth, but it was not. The British had some embarrassing defeats and had to assemble an army of half a million men. About 40 per cent of these who volunteered to fight were found to be too unfit to be soldiers and, although this was actually about the same proportion of infirmity as in industrial areas of France and Germany, British government and public opinion did not see it from this angle. As one Liberal MP put it, 'Empire cannot be built on rickety and flat chested citizens.'

Concern about national efficiency

Performance in the Boer War added to existing worries about 'national efficiency'. Britain no longer had the lead in industry and trade that she enjoyed in the mid-nineteenth century. Inefficiency in war showed the need for better education, welfare and administration. British bungling contrasted with the military and economic efficiency of Germany, where the state was much more fully involved in education and welfare.

Was there pressure from the working class?

Moves towards democracy under the Second and Third Reform Acts also brought a change in the role of the state. Much suspicion of government in the early and mid-nineteenth century was based on how the *aristocracy* was running it. Now power was shifting, as Chapter 4 describes, and a mass *working-class* electorate could ensure the government was used to help the people rather than a wealthy elite. Joseph Chamberlain, as a left-wing Liberal, put the argument clearly following the Third Reform Act: 'Government is the organised expression of the wishes and wants of the people, and under these circumstances let us cease to regard it with suspicion . . . Now it is our business to extend its functions, and to see in what ways its operation can be usefully enlarged.'

Conservative and Liberal politicians often saw social reform as the way to get working-class votes and stop the spread of *socialism*. A writer on the Conservative *Quarterly Review* in 1891 saw social reform as the only way to 'justify to the people the existing basis of society'. Lloyd George repeatedly warned Liberals of the need to meet 'the legitimate claims of labour' to avoid the British Liberal party being replaced by some Labour alternative. It is hard to see parties winning elections because of their promises on social reform, though a number of Liberal candidates opposing laws for an 8-hour maximum working day gained notably worse results than Liberals supporting it in 1892.

Many late nineteenth-century social reforms were apparently unpopular. Housing acts first concentrated on demolishing slums which provided cheap working-class homes and did little to encourage cheap house building. Education and factory acts stopped children working, forced them into school and often compelled their parents to pay school fees. Not surprisingly, laws imposing restrictions and charges were unpopular, and only when they brought obvious benefits like old-age pensions did they get much support. As a Devon fisherman put it in 1911: 'We wants more money and they gives us more laws.'

Politicians saw that the state must ensure workers benefited from growing national wealth and that, in Churchill's words, 'the people demanded something more than liberty'. Social investigators found what they called a 'residuum' at the poorest end of the population made up of unemployed or unemployable people who often turned to crime. The state must stop this group growing and ensure 'respectable' working men did not turn to violent demonstrations, as they did in London in 1886 and 1887. Chamberlain, in government in 1886, encouraged local councils to lay on public works schemes to prevent 'public sentiment' going 'wholly over to the unemployed' and so that the government could still be 'very strict with the loafer or confirmed pauper'.

New state welfare measures were introduced across a range of wealthier countries from the 1870s as governments faced expectations and dangers from a growing working class. Individual reforms had a mixed reception from the public, but national efficiency, democracy and public order all meant that the state must help the poor.

New thinking in economics

Changes in political and economic theory accompanied and encouraged the changes in politics and economic life. Leading economists responded to what they saw as failures in a free market system. W. S. Jevons noted how trade slumps threw 'whole towns and classes of people' into poverty, and Alfred Marshall argued that state action was often better than individual responses at bringing about improvements. These economists' responses used the theory of marginal utility in explaining price movements. The value of each item would depend on how useful an extra one would be to any particular person. This approach to economics also emphasised how £1 extra meant much more to a poor person than to a rich one and encouraged theorists to think about redistributing wealth.

New Liberalism

These ideas fitted in with a changing approach among many political thinkers started by the Oxford philosopher T. H. Green. Green stressed the importance of what he called 'positive' freedom – the freedom to do something – rather than just being free from outside interference. A man benefited little from such negative freedom if he were ill, starving or homeless. Green and later writers, who developed a so-called 'New Liberalism', also viewed government aims in a different way from most mid-nineteenth-century thinkers. These had tended to assess government policy by adding up the effects on lots of individuals, and utilitarians thought they could make precise calculations about this. The New Liberal thinkers saw individuals achieving happiness and fulfilment through being part of a community, and it was necessary to think of society as a whole rather than lots of separate people. Early twentieth-century writers, like J. A. Hobson, thought in these organic terms; the social whole or organism was greater than the sum of the individuals who made it up, and the government must think of the community.

Not all the New Liberal thinkers went this far, but they encouraged a different approach in government. The state needed to guarantee its citizens some sort of minimum standard of living if they were to have 'positive' freedom and proper standards of right and wrong, and lead fulfilling lives. A free market economy allowed some individuals to get too much power and wealth at the expense of others, and the government needed to curb their influence and redistribute some of their money. New Liberal theorists undoubtedly had influence. T. H. Green was a Liberal activist and the Oxford tutor to the future prime minister Asquith. J. A. Hobson and L. T. Hobhouse were politicians whose ideas circulated in newspapers and among left-wing MPs. Yet it would be wrong to suggest simply that new theories led to new reforms. The thinkers were often responding to an existing political debate sparked off in turn by practical problems.

Some reform ideas were developed from earlier thinkers; the Fabian socialists who influenced many politicians believed in the kind of systematic social investigations suggested by utilitarians (see p. 62). Government officials, like Sir Robert Morant at the Education Department, pushed forward new measures as a response to obvious needs. Foreign measures – like the introduction of old-age pensions in Denmark and New Zealand – suggested what could be done in Britain, and the Liberals, who introduced many reforms in government, knew they were acting in a very competitive political world. Late nineteenth-century Conservatives were generally individualist in approach with a strong belief in free market economics, but in the early twentieth century many took up an alternative policy of *protection* – taxes on imported goods which would encourage people to buy British or empire products. These might help provide more jobs for the unemployed and more money for social reform. Both parties were suggesting a bigger role for the state and different answers to working-class problems.

The role of local government

Central government might be getting big ideas, but in 1867 it still relied on a mass of local boards and councils to carry most of them out. As time went on local authorities found they had more legal duties and more jobs they could do if they wished. Many also gained additional powers by special acts of parliament for their own local area. The one big check on what they could do was money. Local government spending was rising faster than central government's, but it could only use one type of tax – rates levied on the value of property. High rates were unpopular, and councils relied more and more on national government grants and loans, which made it easier for ministers and civil servants to tell them what to do.

In 1867 local tasks were carried out by a mass of different boards – highway boards, burial boards, poor law guardians and boards of health – as well as by *borough* councils and *magistrates*. A set of school boards was established in 1870, and then the process stopped. A royal commission criticised the chaos of having different boards administering different areas and levying different rates. The Local Government Board was created in 1871 to help co-ordinate services on a national basis, but it had power to advise rather than instruct local authorities. New county councils took over some powers in 1888, and the 1894 Local Government Act created district councils which took over others. Separate school boards remained until 1902 and poor law guardians until 1929, but the modern pattern of elected local councils controlling local services was largely established by 1900. The new London County Council was soon developing ambitious housing, transport and education schemes.

The role of the state

Defence

National government's first duty remained the defence of the country and, with scares about naval rivalry in the early twentieth century, it became an increasingly costly one. Defence took about 3 per cent of national production and around a quarter of overall government expenditure.

Law and order

The government's next basic responsibility – maintaining law and order – was still managed locally by county police forces which varied in organisation and grew in numbers. England and Wales had an average of 1 policeman for every 731 people by 1891 – lower than earlier and higher than just after the Second World War. Early police forces concentrated on patrolling the streets rather than finding criminals. The Metropolitan Police's detective department – the defective department, as one magazine called it – developed slowly until three of its four chief inspectors were found guilty of corruption, and it was replaced by the Criminal Investigation Department (CID) in 1878. County police forces then gradually established detective sections. The central government took over control of prisons in 1877 but sent offenders under 16 to voluntarily run 'reformatory schools' before state 'borstals' were built from 1907. Irish terrorism led to the beginnings of the Special Branch in 1883 – the start of a 'political police' who search out people threatening the government.

Before the First World War, even village policemen were sometimes instructed to be on the look-out for German spies. In 1909 the chief constable of the East Riding of Yorkshire was enquiring: 'Are any "Foreigners" ever seen in your district, such as "Organ Grinders", "Waiters", or servants of any kind, "Bandsmen", travelling "Photographers", or in fact "Foreigners" of any class or acting in any capacity?'

Official secrets acts in 1889 and 1911 introduced general bans on leaking information from the civil service, and twentieth-century restrictions on immigration began with the loosely enforced Aliens Act in 1905 to stop poverty-stricken or otherwise undesirable foreigners coming into the country.

Religion and education

The state continued to support *Anglican* churches in England and Wales and the Church of Scotland, but the Anglican Church of Ireland was disestablished, losing its estates and tax-collecting powers in 1869. The Church of Wales was later disestablished, by an act of 1914 not carried out until 1920, but in England close ties between state and church remained with church officials in each parish having a part in local administration. T. H. S. Escott described the situation in 1885: 'The squire is a magistrate; not improbably the rector is a magistrate too . . . The parish clerk, beadle, and sexton have all of them a legal and civil status.'[2]

The Church of England still ran many schools, but a state school system was gradually introduced between 1870 and 1914. The Education Act 1870 was designed to 'fill up the gaps' in a patchwork of independently run, mainly religious schools across the country. The locally elected school boards established to do this gradually built up a state system of so-called 'elementary' schools, which taught the basic elements of learning and were the equivalent of modern primary schools. They developed on a fee-paying basis, though by 1891 children from poorer families had their school fees paid from the rates. In England and Wales children were gradually compelled to attend, and the school-leaving age was raised in stages – it was 12 by 1899, and by 1914 about half the children stayed on to 14. An act for Scotland had introduced wider school board control and compulsory attendance earlier, in 1872.

The Victorians generally thought of different education systems for different classes, and secondary or university education was appropriate for the middle and upper classes; in the late nineteenth century a very small number of poorer children – perhaps four or five in a thousand – might win scholarships to pay for their progress to secondary school and university. The state made more general arrangements for secondary schooling in an act of 1902 which allowed county councils to establish their own grammar schools, and in regulations of 1907 to get council and independently run grammar schools to reserve a quarter of their places for elementary school pupils from the poorer classes. The government still played little part in university education – the £100,000 the state put into it in 1905 was about the cost of a single naval frigate.

Health

The state did set up a uniform system for improving public health in the 1870s. The Public Health Act 1872 ensured every part of the country would have a sanitary authority with a medical officer of health. The Public Health Act 1875 clearly stated their duties to provide what we regard as basic services – laying on water supplies, providing sewerage systems, paving and lighting the streets – and the Local Government Board established in 1871 was to supervise all this. The actual functioning of the system was not necessarily as comprehensive. The Local Government Board's medical department overseeing the 1,500 authorities had about ten staff; medical officers of health were appointed gradually and often understood that they would be more popular and were more likely to be reappointed by their local authority if they did not do too much or give property owners much trouble.

It was often difficult to enforce health regulations. Food adulteration acts gave local authorities power to take legal action, but much depended on how good their scientific analysis was. The 1876 Rivers Pollution Act allowed them to clean up rivers, but not if it would interfere with industry, and the government had still not decided on chemical tests for water quality by the First World War.

Individual medical care increased, but rather haphazardly. The 1875 act allowed local authorities to pay for hospital building from the rates; poor law authorities set up medicine dispensaries as well as hospitals and could give medical treatment to patients without their losing their voting rights because of their being labelled *paupers* from 1885, but most was done in large towns and the amount of care varied.

Housing

The state also started providing housing between 1867 and 1914, though on a very small scale. A series of acts between 1868 and 1890 encouraged local councils to pull down slums, but the emphasis was on demolition and rebuilding was left to private enterprise.

Housing of the working classes acts in 1885 and 1890 allowed councils to build homes as long as they charged rents which covered their costs. The central government would provide loans, and laws in 1903 and 1909 gave it power to force councils to start working-class housing schemes. Council house building had begun, and the London County Council built the first large modern council estates in the 1890s. Across Britain only 2 per cent of houses were publicly owned before 1909, and rents were not subsidised until after the First World War.

The 1909 Housing and Town Planning Act gave local councils power to plan future building development; the government was beginning to see planning as an important responsibility and housing as a public service.

Poverty and Liberal welfare reforms

By the early twentieth century the government was becoming more concerned about the overall problem of poverty. This was partly a matter of greater knowledge and a growing guilt feeling in the upper classes. In the nineteenth century there was a stream of novels and commentaries about the hardships of working-class industrial life and how dreadful city slums were. By 1900 the knowledge was becoming more direct and more carefully researched. Many young men at university went to live in town slums as part of the late nineteenth-century 'settlement movement', and almost all the *civil servants* and younger politicians associated with early twentieth-century social reforms had this kind of experience. Seebohm Rowntree's study of poverty in York was more systematic and detailed than ever before, and it showed over half the families in unavoidable poverty there in 1899 had a chief breadwinner in work, but at low wages. People involved in politics became more aware of the problem of poverty and that the poor often could not do much to help themselves.

The Liberals in government from 1905 were most involved in tackling this problem and, not surprisingly, their motives were mixed. Historians have generally favoured three main lines of explanation:

1 Many Liberals thought they had a duty to tackle the problem and believed in the ideas of New Liberalism (see pp. 75–76). The government therefore should set about ensuring minimum living standards because it was the right thing to do.
2 It was too dangerous not to do anything. Without improvements Britain could not increase its national efficiency, and workers might turn to socialism and even revolution. Some employers were pushing for welfare reform – for example at Birmingham, where the Chamber of Commerce put forward varying schemes from 1906 – and their interest can be linked to economic needs.
3 Liberals realised some social reform could be popular. They needed to safeguard their working-class support, especially when Labour candidates were winning by-elections in 1907–08. Churchill, as a Liberal minister in 1908, saw that a social programme 'would not merely benefit the state but fortify the party'. Lloyd George put it very clearly in a letter to his brother about the 1908 budget, which included old-age pensions: 'It is time we did something that appealed straight to the people – it will, I think, help stop this electoral rot, and that is most necessary.'

Reform was necessary, then, but how was it to be done? There was a national system for helping the poor – a centralised and nationally constructed system based on central government supervision and a kind of local democratic control. This poor law administration had been created in 1834 and continued until 1929. It had shown some flexibility, developing to the nearest Britain had to a state health system before the First World War and improving the treatment of poor children and old people in the later nineteenth century. The problem was that it was hated. It was associated with humiliation because paupers were meant to feel that they had failed, normally losing their voting rights. A system designed to brand poor people as social failures could not administer welfare in an increasingly democratic society. The problem was psychological rather than managerial. It meant that the one national organisation which might be used for a co-ordinated attack on poverty was unusable. Instead, the problems were tackled in a piecemeal way by a series of reforms using different organisations and sources of money.

Money was the key problem. By the early twentieth century local authorities were spending about as much as central government. High rates were now a major grievance as they were the only way different local councils and boards could get funds, apart from central government grants and loans. If ratepayers would not stand for large increases, the government had to find other means. Local authorities had generally been in charge of tackling social problems under nineteenth-century acts, but they were only to carry out three of the Liberal government's twelve main social reform laws in 1906–14. The state created a national system for pensions and health care rather than relying on local bodies – which some see as the beginnings of a later 'welfare state'.

Children's welfare

Early measures to help children depended at first on local action and funding. A law in 1906 allowed local councils to decide whether to provide school meals and use ratepayers' money to make them free to poor children. About 350,000 children were eating the school dinners by 1912, though most councils had not yet introduced them. In 1914 the government went further, forcing councils which ran schools to provide meals and promising money to help pay for them.

School medical services came in a similarly gradual way. Councils had to carry out medical inspections on children from 1907 but might or might not provide treatment for the illnesses they found. From 1912 the central government offered some money for treatment and about two-thirds of councils were providing it by 1914.

Local councils and courts also had duties to protect children against their parents. The Children's Act 1908 gave courts, local councils and poor law boards responsibilities to investigate cruelty and look after children where necessary.

Old-age pensions

Old-age pensions were really the key issue for central government. They were seriously discussed in Britain from the 1870s and had been introduced in a few countries, including Germany and New Zealand, before 1900. As Lloyd George saw, they might well win votes, but who was to pay for them? Should people at work contribute, as in Germany, or should the government find the money, as in New Zealand? If workers paid for the pensions, they could hardly be given straightaway to the poor old people who needed them but had not contributed. Yet there were not going to be many votes in a scheme which meant workers making immediate payments and brought no immediate benefit to anybody. The alternative was costly. The government would have to find the money for new benefits, and taxpayers might criticise how the money was spent. Many people saved for their old age; should the others who might have been idlers or have wasted their money on drink now get state hand-outs? On the other hand, could many working people, whom Rowntree's survey showed living near the 'poverty line', ever afford to save much for their old age?

The scheme introduced by Asquith in 1908 was a compromise between these views. The pensions were paid out of government money and given to old people over 70 who needed them. They were only 5 shillings (25p) a week, about 2s less than Rowntree thought could keep an individual person going at subsistence level. If people already had an income over 8s (40p) a week (£21 a year) they would get less, and if it were over 12s (60p) a week (£31 a year) they would get nothing at all. If they had failed to work according to their 'ability, opportunity or need', they were also to get nothing, but this restriction would be hard for any official to assess and was scarcely applied until it was abandoned in 1919.

The pension helped poor old people by giving them something to get by and boosting small savings. They got the money as a right, without the humiliating questions which officials asked before handing out poor relief. The pensions were popular, but they cost a lot of money, and the financial problems Lloyd George had as chancellor of the exchequer convinced him that he must find some other way of financing health care.

Health insurance

The 1911 National Insurance Act was another compromise. It was based on the insurance principle that a worker should make regular payments to get benefits in time of need, but the government and employers added to their contributions so that employees got 9d (about 4p) worth of health insurance by paying 4d (about 2p) a week. Many workers already insured through friendly societies, profit-making commercial insurance companies or trade unions. The government agreed that these should continue to run the insurance scheme, but on government terms. The state decided the payments and basic benefits and compelled all workers earning under £160 a year to join. It combined individual contributions with government subsidy and supervision – a Liberal answer to how the state should care for its citizens while ensuring they had to help themselves. The limited benefits certainly left plenty of room for self-help. Workers who were ill got 10s (50p) a week – Rowntree calculated that over £1 was necessary to keep an average family – and the payments continued only for 26 weeks. The scheme provided free health care by local doctors (general practitioners or GPs) but little hospital care and no dental or eye treatment, and it was provided only for the worker who paid insurance contributions, not other members of the family. Lloyd George called the scheme an 'ambulance wagon'; it helped meet emergencies when a worker was ill, but was not a national health service like the one started after the Second World War.

The state and unemployment

It was easy to see that people became ill through no fault of their own and deserved help. Unemployment was different. From the late nineteenth century economists and social investigators were offering a variety of reasons why people often could not find work, and government ministers became more worried about what the unemployed would do. People receiving help from the poor rates could not vote, but they could cause disturbances and might win popular sympathy. At first ministers encouraged local councils to provide work for the unemployed when their numbers increased in economic slump. Chamberlain did this in a ministerial circular in 1886, though without providing any money to help. In 1905 the Unemployed Workmen's Act encouraged town councils to start work schemes and set up labour exchanges, but civil servants soon concluded that these were not very effective. If large numbers were unemployed in a trade slump it would be more difficult to find money from local rates to develop public works schemes, and local labour exchanges could only give information on local vacancies.

From 1908 the two most enthusiastic New Liberal ministers, Lloyd George and Churchill, had the two key government posts, in charge of financial and industrial policies as chancellor of the exchequer and president of the Board of Trade respectively, and they started central government action over unemployment. The Development Act 1909 provided state money to create jobs in the countryside, not through the government's own schemes but by helping to finance others.

Labour exchanges

By 1910 the government created a national system of labour exchanges. Most obviously they were an efficient way of helping workers to find jobs and employers to find workers. To some extent they succeeded as over 3,000 people a day were finding employment in them by 1914, though looking at it another way only a quarter of those who came for jobs in 1910–14 got them.

Labour exchanges were more than an administrative arrangement. Churchill thought they would give labourers more dignity as they would not have to trudge round to employers as if they were begging for work. Trade union officials suspected they would help employers get labour to break strikes. Civil servants saw they were a way of collecting useful government statistics and would help in setting up an unemployment insurance scheme, which was what Churchill and Lloyd George saw as their next measure.

Unemployment insurance

Unemployment insurance, introduced under the 1911 National Insurance Act, was to be paid for, like health insurance, with contributions from workers, employers and the government. In this way it was subsidised and seemed to be treating unemployment as a misfortune, like sickness, but there were all kinds of restrictions. The benefits were small and very short term – 7s (35p) a week for up to 15 weeks – and they were not paid to employees who had been dismissed or were out of work because of strikes. Most importantly, the scheme covered under a quarter of the workforce of over 10 million, mainly those who were in jobs particularly affected by short-term unemployment because of trade slumps.

Working conditions and labour relations

Working conditions and wages

Whereas unemployment benefits were a new feature in the twentieth century, factory workers' hours were generally controlled by 1867. The law restricted only women's and children's hours, but in practice this meant limiting men's work as well, as they could not normally run the factories alone. The regulations were extended in the late nineteenth century with more government inspectors to enforce them. From 1878 workshops with under 50 employees were inspected like factories. Young shop workers' hours were limited from 1886, and the first law to limit men's hours was introduced in 1893. This act allowing the government to restrict railwaymen's work time was designed for safety, but a law in 1908 introduced a maximum 8-hour day for all coal miners. There was a range of laws to improve employees' safety and another series of acts between 1880 and 1906 gave workers greater rights to compensation from their employers for injuries at work.

Laws concerning working hours and safety were necessary for workers' health, but it was quite a different matter for the state to fix wages. This had not been done since the early nineteenth century, and politicians generally accepted that wages should be decided by bargaining between employers and workers in a free labour market. Many of the arguments were similar to those about introducing a minimum wage in the 1990s. Forcing employers to pay higher wages would push up costs, deter them from using as many workers and create unemployment. On the other hand, minimum wages might produce a better-fed, healthier, more efficient labour force with more money to spend, increasing demand for goods which, in turn, would create more jobs.

Beside the economic arguments were beliefs about how far the state should guarantee a minimum income for its citizens. New Liberal thinkers and politicians generally believed the state should, so that people could lead full lives, but Liberal ministers did not consider they ought to decide the appropriate wage rates in different industries. The Trade Boards Act of 1909 was designed to fix wages in so-called sweated industries where workers were underpaid, but it was to be done by boards of employer and worker representatives with a few independent members. The government would then enforce what they had decided. At the start trade boards covered under 200,000 workers, but this rose to about half a million by 1914. Wage rates largely remained a matter for bargains between employers and workers at the start of the First World War, but the 1909 act and another in 1912 were important moves away from the free market.

Labour relations

The state's approach to labour relations was transformed between 1867 and 1914. Governments chosen by a mainly working-class electorate had to respond when workers had problems with their employers. Furthermore, trade unions grew massively from under 1 million members in 1867 to around 4 million in 1914 and largely financed a Labour party which threatened to win support from Liberals or Conservatives. When it had 30 MPs after the 1906 election, it was able to gain a new law which increased trade unions' power by putting them outside normal legal restrictions as long as they were not responsible for crimes or strikes against the community. There were serious strikes at times from the late 1880s onwards, and the Miners' Federation of Great Britain and the National Union of Railwaymen formed in 1913 could control the coal and trains on which

Britain's economy depended before the First World War. How was the government to respond?

One way was military action, which Liberal governments used with fatal effect. They sent a gunboat to deal with Hull dockers in 1893, and troops involved with coal strikes in Yorkshire and South Wales killed miners in 1893 and 1911. In the long run repression was embarrassing for Liberals who wanted worker support, and difficult to use in a democracy.

The main emphasis was on negotiating settlements, normally by mediation – which involved people outside a dispute bringing the two sides together – and occasionally by arbitration, where an outsider made a decision. Ministers occasionally mediated in important disputes from 1893 when Lord Rosebery, as foreign secretary, settled a miners' strike. Lloyd George, who apparently had an incomparable capacity to be all things to all men, stopped rail strikes in 1907 and 1911. In the more normal way the Board of Trade's Labour Department, established in 1893, would be called in to help. The Labour Department busied itself collecting a range of statistics on production, prices and wages which would help in suggesting deals in line with current market rates. Under the 1896 Conciliation Act it could mediate or arbitrate in a dispute if the two sides requested it. In 1912 the special Industrial Council was also set up to arbitrate when both sides agreed to its making a decision. The Industrial Council was not much used, but government conciliation was. From the 1890s the state took up a mediating or peace-making role between unions and employers to stop strikes and keep the country moving. It was the beginning of the three-way relationship which developed much further after 1914 and was used until Thatcher's Conservative government came to power in 1979.

Economic and financial reform

Taxation

With growing defence and welfare costs, how to pay for state action was a major question by the early 1900s, and the two main parties gave different answers. Conservatives thought that charging taxes on imports was the solution. This would not only provide money, but also protect British workers' jobs by encouraging people to buy home-produced goods rather than foreign ones – what was known as a policy of protection.

Liberal thinkers had another approach. Firstly, they believed in taking more money from those who did not work for it. Death duties on wealth people inherited were one way; a Conservative government introduced these in 1889, but Liberal chancellors of the exchequer increased them to 20 per cent on large amounts by 1914. Taxing unearned income more heavily than earned was another way, and Asquith started this as chancellor in 1907. The most controversial was plans to tax land values presented by Lloyd George in his 1909 and 1914 budgets but never fully carried out.

Liberals also believed in using taxes to redistribute wealth more equally in the population by taking a larger proportion of income from rich people than poor ones – what is called progressive taxation. This was seen in several Liberal budgets, but particularly Lloyd George's 'people's budget' of 1909, which introduced an extra super-tax on higher incomes. Whereas taxes on ordinary goods were likely to come from rich and poor alike, what were known as direct taxes on income, land or inheritance could be designed to hit the wealthy rather than the workers. Before the First World War income tax fell only on the middle and upper class. The proportion of government income from direct taxation rose from 44 per cent to 60 per cent between 1888 and 1914. While mid-nineteenth-century governments had tried to keep their spending down, twentieth-century governments were deliberately taxing the rich more heavily, not only to defend the country but to finance services like pensions and health insurance for the poor and working class.

The land question

The new approach to taxes reflected a changing view of private property and land ownership. Left-wing politicians saw land as a resource for the community rather than as a sacrosanct piece of private property, and the state's treatment of landownership was changing. This went furthest in Ireland where tenants gained extensive rights in their land in 1881 – safeguards against being turned out of their holdings and the right to have their rents fixed by government-appointed tribunals instead of landlords. Here the state was transferring rights from landlords to tenants. Highland crofters gained a similar deal in Scotland in 1886. The state went much further in Ireland in a series of Conservative government measures subsidising backward areas in the 1890s and lending vast sums at specially low interest rates so that tenants could buy their farms. Most Irish tenants bought their land on terms laid down in Wyndham's Act in 1903 and a later law of 1909. Land reform in England did not go very far. Laws in 1887 and 1890 allowed local councils to buy land for allotments where workers might grow food. Little was done, but the land question was a vital issue in English politics. Lloyd George planned a substantial transfer of rights and ownership in his Land Campaign of 1913–14.

Economic activity

In one form or another the state was also running more services and controlling more enterprises. Local councils took over gas, electricity, water and tramway companies, sometimes using general laws like the 1870 Tramways Act but more normally obtaining special local acts. By 1888 councils owned over a quarter of the country's tramway mileage and supplied nearly half the gas consumers. These were services which people increasingly saw as necessities and where little competition was possible. Many therefore argued that it was better for local authorities to control them rather than private monopolists.

In addition to the Post Office, which it had always run, the central government took over the telegraph system in 1869. The Post Office gained an effective monopoly control of the telephone network in 1912. The state had for a long time run some naval dockyards and arsenals and, as it spent more on defence, it gave more contracts to shipbuilders and arms manufacturers. It also made some foreign investments in connection with Britain's imperial interests, buying shares in the Suez Canal in 1875 and the Anglo-Persian Oil Company in 1914.

Historians have sometimes argued that in 1867 the British state did the minimum possible amount. No one could argue convincingly that this was true in 1914. After the Second World War Britain developed a welfare state which looked after its citizens from the cradle to the grave and redistributed wealth by progressive taxation. Government ministers managed the economy and intervened in industrial disputes, negotiating with trade union leaders and industrialists. The beginnings of these developments were clear before the First World War, but how far had they progressed? Was Britain still a free market economy where the government just made alterations as necessity demanded? Or was it a state with a new collectivist approach which the government used to try to transform society?

Document case study

Why Lloyd George introduced national health insurance in 1911

6.1 Lloyd George's public view in 1908

Lloyd George's comments in The Daily News, *27 August 1908, after his return from a visit to Germany*

I never realised before on what a gigantic scale the German pension scheme is conducted. Nor had I any idea how successfully it works. I had read much about it, but no amount of study at home . . . can convey to the mind a clear idea of all that state insurance means to Germany . . . It touches the great mass of German people in well-nigh every walk of life. Old-age pensions form but a comparatively small part of the system. Does the German worker fall ill? State insurance comes to his aid. Is he invalided from work? Again he gets a regular grant whether he has reached the pension age or not.

Source: E. P. Hennock, 'The origins of British national insurance and the German precedent 1880–1914', in W. J. Mommsen (ed.), *The emergence of the welfare state in Britain and Germany 1850–1950*, London, 1981, p. 87

6.2 A radical Liberal MP urges Lloyd George to take action

H. Spender in The Contemporary Review, *January 1909*

[Lloyd George should take] a leaf from the book of Bismarck who dealt the heaviest blow against German socialism not by his laws of oppression . . . but by that great system of state insurance which now safeguards the German work-man at almost every point of his industrial career.

Source: B. B. Gilbert, *The evolution of national insurance in Great Britain: the origins of the welfare state*, London, 1966, p. 257

6.3 A civil servant explains the origins of the reforms

W. J. Braithwaite, a civil servant who advised Lloyd George and visited Germany to collect information, describes the thinking behind the reform in his memoirs

There were, however, other personal matters in L.G.'s experience [in addition to royal commission reports on the poor laws] which certainly had weighed heavily with him and which caused him to go on with insurance.

First there was his experience with the Old Age Pensions Act of 1908 . . . This had taught him what the cost of free grants could be, and turned his mind to contributory insurance.

Next, L.G. was influenced by his tour or tours in Germany. He had been there in 1908 with a party of 'Young Liberals' and had been very much impressed with the best side of everything which had been shown him. Social insurance had then been going in Germany for some twenty-five years.

And lastly he had been very much attracted by the anti-consumption campaign. He had seen the sanatoria in Germany. The yearly total of deaths through consumption was horrifying. He was suffering from a sore throat himself, and some people whispered that he was afraid he had consumption . . .

These personal matters, then, in L.G.'s own experience were contributory factors of great importance. In fact I don't think he had taken any real interest in the Poor Law Report: it was not till the bill was well on its way that so far as I know he started looking at it, and I gathered that he had not read a word of it before . . . He himself came thus to the insurance question from his own experience, and he must accordingly have the credit (or discredit) of national contributory insurance . . .

Source: H. N. Bunbury (ed.), *Lloyd George's ambulance wagon. Being the memoirs of William J. Braithwaite, 1911–1912*, London, 1957, pp. 70–72

6.4 W. J. Braithwaite

German methods of officialdom and compulsion . . . were awful warnings to me. Something simpler and more self-working must, I thought, be found for England.

Source: H. N. Bunbury (ed.) *Lloyd George's ambulance wagon*, quoted in E. P. Hennock, 'The origins of British national insurance and the German precedent, 1880–1914' in W. J. Mommsen (ed.), *The emergence of the welfare state*, pp. 111–12

Document case-study questions

1 What are the different reasons given in these documents for the introduction of national health insurance?

2 How reliable are (a) Lloyd George's own public statement in Document 6.1 and (b) the civil servant's memoirs in Document 6.3 as evidence of Lloyd George's motives?

3 How useful is the comment in Document 6.2?

4 What do these documents suggest was the relative importance of the German example and other factors in the development of national health insurance? Consider the different reasons for Lloyd George's introduction of insurance and how they were connected.

Notes and references

1 P. K. O'Brien, 'Taxation 1688–1914', *History Review*, no. 27, March 1997.

2 T. H. S. Escott, *England: its people, polity and pursuits*, 1885, cited in B. Harrison, *The transformation of British politics 1860–1995*, Oxford, 1996.

7 The growth of corporatism and welfare provision, 1914–1945

The government did far more to provide welfare services and regulate the economy from 1914. This was partly because of war needs, but there were other complex reasons, and there has been much criticism of government responses in the 1920s and 1930s.

How and why did the role of the state expand?

What the state did and what its citizens expected it to do were transformed between 1914 and 1945. The number of *civil servants* increased from 282,000 in 1914 to 387,000 in 1939 and to over 500,000 following the Second World War. Government spending grew from under 12 per cent of Gross Domestic Product (GDP)* before the First World War to 26 per cent in 1937 and 37 per cent in the later 1940s. War costs, particularly interest payments on money borrowed to fight, account for part of this, but not all. The government spent a growing proportion of national wealth in peacetime even when it was able to reduce its interest payments. Whereas its spending had increased by only 1 per cent (adjusted to allow for price increases) between 1900 and 1913, it grew by 8.5 per cent between 1920 and 1934.

The government had to spend more because people now thought it had more responsibilities. It was widely believed that the poor and the sick had a right to help and that the government should not only run its own budget but manage the country's economy to achieve full employment and prosperity. Why did the state's role grow so rapidly?

War

The government had so much more to do in the First and Second World Wars that changing wartime needs and attitudes are the most obvious answer to the question. Twentieth-century wars, unlike earlier ones, affect the whole population, and the extent of their impact has been strongly disputed by historians. How people's attitudes changed is particularly difficult for historians to assess, no doubt because responses were varied and how people thought in wartime might be very different from how they felt a few years later. Some historians have stressed that war produced a sense of togetherness and a general

---

* The total national wealth produced in the country, as compared to GNP (Gross National Product), which includes income from overseas investments.

agreement or consensus that more welfare measures were necessary for less fortunate citizens. This argument is strongest in the Second World War, when evacuation of children from cities, mass bombing and rationing helped give people a sense of common struggle. Men from different classes 'rubbing shoulders' in the army and town children going to live with country families meant that very varied people found out more about each other and perhaps cared more about each other – developing what is termed a sense of 'social solidarity'.[1]

There are, of course, alternative interpretations of the wars' effects. More knowledge of other people could generate distrust or disgust as much as a sense of common purpose. More state regulation could produce a dislike of 'red tape' rather than an acceptance of government intervention. Victory could be taken as showing a society's strength rather than exposing a need for reform, and twentieth-century war was so costly and involved so much borrowing that it was difficult to afford welfare improvements afterwards.

Whatever the long-term effects, war certainly led to more government regulation in the short term, and this extended beyond managing the economy for the war effort to giving greater attention to citizens' health. After all, a fit workforce was specially important in war, and children seemed more precious when so many young people were losing their lives. As the inscription on the first free issue of cod liver oil in the Second World War put it, 'the raw material of the race is too valuable to be put at risk'. *Working-class* men risking their lives for their country perhaps had to be offered a better deal afterwards, or at least promised some improvement at the end, as Lloyd George understood when he spoke of 'homes fit for heroes' in 1918. Certainly the government developed large-scale reconstruction programmes in the later stages of both world wars, but here the experience was very different. To a great extent the programmes at the end of the Second World War were carried out and those from the First World War were not. The First World War led to the Ministry of Labour in 1916, the Ministry of Reconstruction in 1917 and the Ministry of Health in 1919, but the reconstruction ministry did not last long and the others were weak. Ambitious programmes drawn up in 1917–19 were largely abandoned when economies were required in 1921–22.

Fear of revolution

Fear of revolution might be a stronger motive for reform than gratitude to the returning soldiers. Russia had a communist revolution in 1917, and there were left-wing risings in Germany and Hungary in 1918–19. Fear of some similar unrest apparently lay behind the two major welfare improvements which did follow the war. An 'out-of-work donation', much larger than earlier state benefits, was given to soldiers and war workers when they lost their jobs in 1918, and its generous terms distorted arrangements for unemployment insurance through the 1920s. Unrest in major cities, particularly Glasgow, led to government controls on rents during the war and was undoubtedly one reason for the 1919 Housing Act (see document case study). Later, unemployment benefit was given on stricter and sometimes more humiliating terms in the 1920s and 1930s, and the housing programme was cut back drastically in 1921. Worries about revolution declined, but did not quite disappear.

Democracy

Following the 1918 Reform Act Britain was at least near to a democracy (see Chapter 3), and a mainly working-class electorate might well expect a government more active in redistributing wealth and providing welfare. The Labour party had more ambitious welfare plans and formed its first governments, but these were short lived. It did not gain a parliamentary majority to carry out a programme until 1945. The Conservative party dominated British politics between 1918 and 1939 and, although responsible for some important social reform, put much emphasis on keeping taxation and government spending down.

Economic problems and theories

While the nineteenth-century economy, despite ups and downs, had generally been an enormous success story, after the First World War major industries – like coal, iron and cotton – had far greater problems in selling their goods in world markets. Since the British goods were not required or could not be sold at competitive prices, many firms had no alternative but to slim down, close or go bankrupt, and the result was massive *structural unemployment* – people thrown out of work on a long-term basis because the products they made were no longer saleable. Governments were used to thinking that investment and employment were not really their business. They thought that investment should be left to the *free market*; capitalists would identify opportunities to supply goods and services profitably, they would then require more labour and it was up to workers to find the vacancies. This did not seem to be happening, particularly in the world economic slump which followed the Wall Street crash (the collapse of share prices on the American stock exchange) in 1929. Some regions of the country were not recovering from the slump even by the mid-1930s, and there was a case for more government action. Keynes pointed out that money might remain unused in the economy and that the government itself should invest in industry and public works. Although his ideas were not widely accepted or even fully formulated until 1936, a number of progressives were arguing for greater government investment and initiative. Economic problems and social expectations both demanded more state activity.

The role of the state

Defence

Defence remained the government's first duty, and modern warfare made it the costliest. Paying interest on war debt accounted for around a quarter to a third of government spending through the 1920s. Rearmament pushed up expenditure again in the later 1930s.

Law and order

The state gained more powers which government ministers could use to maintain law and order. The defence of the realm acts, introduced in the First World War and largely ended in 1921, allowed the government to stop normal press freedom or freedom of speech and imprison people without trial if war needs demanded it. The Emergency Powers Act introduced before the Second World War allowed the government to make whatever regulations were necessary for public safety, defence and public order; the home secretary could detain people whom he might reasonably believe had enemy connections, like German refugees.

The Emergency Powers Act 1920 gave ministers the right to use troops during strikes to keep food and fuel supplies moving, and governments declared states of emergency under it in 1921, 1924 and 1926. In exceptional circumstances troops might be used to keep order, as at Rochdale in 1931 when there were battles between police and unemployed.

Circumstances in Ireland were always exceptional in the last years of British rule. Martial law, involving military regulations and courts, was introduced after the Easter Rising there in 1916 and in 1920 when there was a full-scale Anglo-Irish war. Early twentieth-century Britain was generally a peaceful country where policemen bicycled through villages or walked round towns on the 'beat', but the state held large – some would say intimidating – powers in reserve.

Religion and morality

Religion was much less important in politics after 1914 than it had been in the nineteenth century. The Church of England and the Church of Scotland have remained established with special rights, but there has been less controversy over their state connections or about how far the government should support a particular type of Christian belief than before 1914.

The state still used public money to support moral views and also limited individual freedom. The British Broadcasting Corporation (BBC), set up in 1926 under royal charter and paid for by radio users' licence fees, preached a clear Christian morality. The new film industry introduced its own system of censorship, knowing that otherwise the state would intervene. Pubs were shut in the afternoon and their hours restricted under First World War regulations and the 1921 Licensing Act – at first to safeguard war production, but with a clear moral purpose. A whole mass of laws prevented homosexual acts in private, betting and prostitution on the streets in public and all kinds of 'indecency' in books and magazines.

Local government

The central government still relied on local councils to carry out its social policies. The Ministry of Health, which took over the old Local Government Board's duties in 1919, sent instructions to county and *borough* councils whose committees ran schools, hospitals and police forces. From 1929 they took on the job of the poor law guardians, distributing money to the poor and certain unemployment benefits. If ministers relied on councils, the councils in turn depended on central government for an increasing part of their income – 25 per cent in 1914, 40 per cent by 1939 and over half soon after the Second World War. Local councils had more to do, but often less freedom to do it. They were increasingly carrying out government policies, following government rules and using government money.

More government money was certainly spent on social services. Whereas spending by central government and local councils on social services had not gone far above 4 per cent of GNP before the First World War, it was always over 8 per cent between the wars. There were sharp cut-backs in 1922 and 1931, and more benefits were given to individuals on the basis of family means tests. Officials would find out about a family's savings and all its members' income before deciding whether to give benefits. It was a way of keeping government spending down and ensuring help went only to those who needed it, but it also meant people lost out because they had saved and officials asked embarrassing questions. There were 18 separate means tests for different benefits by 1939, and they were widely hated. Yet they seemed to offer some means of limiting government spending, which had increased because of large-scale housing and unemployment benefit schemes.

Housing

Housing was one of the government's most urgent problems at the end of the war. Before the First World War private enterprise provided 95 per cent of working-class homes, and there was little council house building. By 1918 there was a massive shortage of houses, and it seemed workers could not afford the sort of rents private builders would have to charge to cover their costs and make a profit. Limits which the government introduced on rents in 1915 made builders even more reluctant to invest in homes for the workers.

The problem after the war might have been left to the free market, as it had generally been before. Presumably workers would have paid more rent and builders would have cut costs to provide cheaper homes, but there would have been a time lag and much discontent. The government could not risk this. People were now used to limited rents, houses were needed quickly, the prime minister promised 'homes fit for heroes', and ministers feared revolution if they did not act (see document case study). Building houses would also provide jobs and help deal with their other main problem – how to cope with large-scale unemployment when soldiers and munitions workers lost their posts at the end of the war.

In 1919 the government therefore brought in two housing laws. One promised local councils government money to build homes beyond what they could raise by a small rate increase (1d in the £ – about 0.4p – assessed on property values). A second gave government subsidies for houses put up by private builders.

The council houses built were good but costly, and apparently more expensive than they need have been. The average cost of building a council house was £838 in 1921 compared with £371 two years later. It is doubtful whether they helped the poor greatly as, even with government subsidies, the rents were high and they were largely taken by skilled labourers or office workers. In 1921 the housing programme was cut back and the building subsidies stopped because the government was spending too much. In many ways worries about balancing the budget and price rises had overtaken fears about working-class disturbances.

State initiatives on housing continued, nevertheless. A Conservative law in 1923 was mainly intended to encourage private house building, and a Labour one in 1924 stimulated council house construction through subsidies which lasted to 1934. Laws in 1930, 1933 and 1935 were designed to get slums cleared, which had been the main intention of housing measures in the nineteenth century. Overall about 1,300,000 council houses were built with government subsidies between 1919 and 1939. Out of a total of over 4 million houses built between the wars, over 40 per cent were put up with the help of state money. About half of the population still lived in privately rented homes at the beginning of the Second World War, but housing was now seen as a government responsibility and the age of mass council housing was well established.

The era of town planning was in its early stages. An act in 1919 required town councils to prepare planning schemes, and the Ministry of Town and Country Planning was set up in 1942, though permission was not needed for all developments until 1947.

Unemployment benefits

How to help the unemployed was an insoluble problem for governments after the First World War. Before the war a small-scale unemployment insurance scheme was set up, but it applied to under a quarter of workers. It only allowed for 7s (35p) a week benefit when an average family needed well over £1, and that would be paid for only 15 weeks. The government had to provide help for large numbers of soldiers and munitions workers who were left without jobs after fighting and toiling for their country. The insurance scheme was little help. Instead the government paid the out-of-work donation, and the amount was decided according to what was necessary for subsistence – reasonably healthy living – for a worker and the family who depended on him. The payments were much more generous than someone would get under the health or unemploy-ment insurance plans; to reward war service and avoid unrest, ministers could hardly do less.

The government did not expect to pay for such generous benefits on a long-term basis. Ministers considered help for the unemployed should be paid for on the insurance principle – people making contributions whilst earning to pay for benefits when out of work. Consequently it introduced a new unemployment insurance scheme in 1920, much wider ranging than the old one and applying to most workers except those in farming, domestic service or jobs where unemployment was very unlikely. As in 1911, it would be financed by workers, employers and government. The benefits might be paid for up to half a year, but workers were required to make six weeks' insurance contributions for every week's benefit money received. The payments would, however, be much more generous than before, providing a decent subsistence for a worker and his dependants.

This sounded fine, but what about men who could not find any jobs so that they could make insurance payments in the first place? What would happen if they were unemployed for more than six months or six times the period they had worked? What calculations had the government made about the likely proportion of workers who would be unemployed and, therefore, the relationship between payments and benefits?

Here plans fell apart. The government calculated just over 5 per cent of workers would be unemployed, but the average in the 1920s and 1930s was about 10 per cent. There was a slump early in the 1920s, and some people did not find a job, so they could not start making contributions. The government wanted to use the insurance principle but must, it seemed, continue paying existing benefits to people who genuinely could not find work. Trying to fit together two requirements which never would fit, the government introduced over 20 laws to distinguish between insurance benefits and others, and unpopular ways were found to cut costs without cutting off the needy and deserving. One way was to find out whether applicants were 'genuinely seeking work'; from 1921 to 1930 people were turned away on nearly 3 million occasions when they could not convince the appropriate officials. As time went on the government had to accept that unemployment benefits would be given for an unlimited period and without the required insurance payments, but it could try to restrict help to those who really could not do without. It used what became known as a household 'means test', enquiring about family savings and whether anybody else in a household earned money. This sort of enquiry, which was used more extensively after 1931, provoked great disgust. Should an unemployed worker get a lower benefit because he had saved a little while in work rather than spending it in the pub and should a father get less for his family because his son did a paper-round?

The government tried to make sense of the unemployment benefit arrangements in 1934 in a law clearly distinguishing between allowances paid under the insurance scheme and others, but anomalies and injustices remained. Those who did get full benefits had gained as prices fell. The Labour chancellor of the exchequer, Philip Snowden, calculated that the unemployed were 36 per cent better off in 1931 than in 1924 and, although benefits were then cut as a result, they were subsequently raised again. Other calculations have suggested that average unemployment benefit in the 1930s would purchase more than an unskilled labourer's wages 25 years earlier. Certainly a man got more money from the state when unemployed than he could get under the national insurance scheme when sick.

Pensions

Old-age pensions were put on to an insurance basis more easily. Pensions had first been given from the start of 1909 as simple payments from the government to poor people over 70 without any contributions to a pension scheme. A new scheme for widows and orphans as well as old-age pensions was introduced in 1925. Workers and employers were to make larger national insurance payments to cover pensions from the age of 65 and, although there was a state subsidy, all pensions would in due course be financed by these contributions. The pensions of 10s (50p) a week would give old people the same kind of living standard as those who got help from the poor law guardians.

Health care

Health care continued to be provided under the 1911 National Insurance Act, which meant it came free only to workers who paid contributions, not their families, and it covered family doctor rather than hospital treatment. As the societies which administered it got more money, they frequently offered to pay for extras like dental treatment and occasionally hospital services. The health care provided was varied and selective, not uniform and available to everybody. The doctors' organisation, the British Medical Association, agreed that insurance cover must be extended and treatment improved. The state scheme did not cover the *middle class* and in illness workers got a fixed benefit whatever the size of their family. Family men would get much more if they were unemployed.

War needs brought incentives for health improvements. Infant clinics, schools for mothers and works canteens sprang up in the First World War. Free orange juice, milk and cod liver oil for babies came in the Second World War, and far more school meals were served up – 1,650,000 a schoolday in 1945 compared with 130,000 in 1940.

There were many different health care organisations – ones for childbirth and child welfare, school medical services, arrangements for family doctors under the national insurance scheme and a variety of hospitals. Some hospitals had been started by the poor law guardians and were taken over by local councils, some had been established by the councils themselves and many of the best were run by voluntary charitable organisations. Health care varied from one locality to another, and seemed a matter of chance rather than planning. There was an obvious and widely debated need for more co-ordination.

This came in the Second World War with the Emergency Medical Service, which included over two-thirds of all British hospitals and gradually cared for more categories of people from injured troops to child evacuees. The government brought out a white paper – a statement of its policy – called 'A national health service' in 1944, outlining how 'a comprehensive service covering every branch of medical and allied activity' should give free treatment. This may suggest that the National Health Service which began in 1948 was already planned. Some kind of universal health service was, but what eventually emerged was the outcome of detailed negotiation – indeed bitter struggle – between the government, doctors and a lot of other interested groups. The National Health Service may be seen as both a logical climax to decades of health care development and a compromise between warring factions.

The Beveridge report and the future of welfare reform

The 'Report on social insurance and allied services' by the economist Sir William Beveridge also came during the war, in 1942. Beveridge was asked to work out a coherent system for financing different benefits to replace the chaos which had developed in the 1930s. Civil servants had already been considering plans for change, and the Labour party favoured both a state health service and social security reform before the Second World War. Beveridge's report suggested that the national insurance system with uniform worker and employer contributions should be used to finance not only sickness and unemployment benefits but also various pensions. The benefits should be the same for everyone and enough for subsistence, keeping people healthy and physically 'efficient'. This system needed to be accompanied by a state health service, family allowances to support children and something near 'full employment' so that those in work could pay for it all.

The report outlined the key features of the welfare state which developed after the Second World War to keep people free from want for any reason and is seen as a significant stage in its creation. On one side it shows how important the New Liberal thinking and reforms before the First World War were in developing the modern system. Beveridge himself was a Liberal. His plans were based on the insurance principle used in 1911 for national insurance and the idea of a minimum living standard, which Liberal thinkers had developed around 1900 and was an important basis for reforms in the 1940s.

The circumstances surrounding the report and its publication also hint at the importance of war and democracy in bringing changes. Beveridge's report recommended the same payments and benefits for all, and this 'universality' may have seemed more appropriate when people were working together and sharing sacrifices in war. Civil servants and government ministers were at first doubtful about carrying it out but, with skilful publicity, Beveridge's plans won great popular support.

Family allowances

One of Beveridge's recommendations, family allowances, was introduced before the war ended. There had been a strong campaign for these payments, based on the number of children in a family, in the 1930s. How far they came because of the campaign or because of wartime concern for children's health and equal treatment is debatable. They were the best means of dealing with the problem of balancing benefits and wages.

Large families sometimes needed extra money just to bring up children to be healthy, and by 1945 the state was expected to provide this. Yet extra money for each child given to people on state benefits could mean that an unemployed man with a large family received more than one in a low-paid job. From the early nineteenth century to the twenty-first the state has been concerned that those in employment should somehow be better off than those not working. The one way of ensuring this while providing necessary help for families was apparently a child allowance paid both to those who were earning and those who were not. It would then be fairly easy to ensure that state benefits to cover a husband's and wife's living costs were below workers' wages. Family allowances can be explained by a mixture of campaigning, wartime sentiments and hard-headed civil service calculations.

Selectivity or universality?

Beveridge's proposals and family allowances show one characteristic of 1940s welfare measures which differed from 1930s ones. In the 1930s benefits were given very selectively, varied a lot and were not always designed to cover living costs fully. There were different arrangements for unemployment benefit depending on a worker's payments and how long he had been out of work. There were varied arrangements for sickness cover – varied between hundreds of societies which administered the scheme – and they only covered some members of a family and some of their needs. Not surprisingly, workers put more money into voluntary or commercial schemes overall than into the state's national insurance. Plans in the 1940s, by contrast, were to be universal – to cover all citizens for all their basic needs. Whatever the reasons, it was a vital change and the key characteristic of what we call a welfare state.

Education

Education changes combined selection and universality. Important reforms came at the end of each world war by laws in 1918 and 1944. The school-leaving age was raised to 14 in 1918 and 15 in 1944. Fees were abolished in elementary schools in 1918 and secondary schools in 1944. More chances were gradually offered to intelligent pupils who could pass the necessary examinations. There were more free places for poorer children in grammar (secondary) schools from 1918, though a number of working-class children still did not take them because of expense, and there were 200 free university places. The 1944 act provided that all children should have secondary education – in grammar schools if they passed the required '11-plus', or else in new secondary modern schools. University education was to be free for those who could gain places – a provision the state has not been able to maintain into the twenty-first century. The 1944 act provided different levels of free education for all who could pass the necessary examinations – not complete equality, but a kind of equal opportunity, and established a meritocracy where, although privileges remained, people could advance by their own efforts and intelligence. How much war helped in achieving this new meritocratic age is doubtful. Education changes had been planned at the start of both wars, and the Second World War actually delayed the raising of the school-leaving age to 15, but the 1918 and 1944 acts were, at least in part, an outcome of wartime social thinking.

Industrial relations and the development of corporatism

Government involvement in relations between employers and workers grew rapidly from the 1890s and became more important from the First World War. What historians and political thinkers call corporatism developed. This comes about when the government works with powerful economic groups, most importantly industrialists and trade unions but also sometimes financiers or traders. Such co-operation seemed necessary both in the First World War, when the government had to ensure maximum production for the war effort, and when strikes threatened the British economy in the years afterwards.

In wartime Lloyd George worked closely with industrialists, encouraging the foundation of the Federation of British Industries in 1916. Ministers made special agreements with trade unions in the munitions industries to avoid strikes and get disputes settled by arbitration. Trade unions, of course, could expect something in return, and there were new minimum wage arrangements. For example, miners had their wages fixed on a national basis as they wanted, rather than regionally as had been agreed in 1912. Even agricultural labourers, who were among the least well-organised workers, gained minimum wages in 1917, although the arrangement did not last. There was an extension of trade boards on which employers' and workers' representatives together with a few government appointees decided wages in low-paid industries. They seemed more necessary when ministers were worried about unrest following the war, and by 1921 they regulated the wages of about 3 million workers compared with a half million in 1914. In 1917 the government's Whitley Committee recommended joint employer–worker councils to discuss wages and conditions and, although they were only established in a few industries, these Whitley councils covered about 3½ million workers by 1921.

Councils and committees in which employers and trade unions could work with the government at a national level were an obvious way of getting co-operation in a time of industrial unrest and a key feature of corporatism. The government backed the National Industrial Conference in 1919, the new Ministry of Labour consulted widely among employers and workers, and an industrial court was established to decide disputes if both parties agreed.

When the government established the Economic Advisory Council in the slump of 1930, it included industrialists and trade unionists, although these were later consulted less when they were likely to put forward their own industry's interests rather than a more national viewpoint.

State regulation of hours and working conditions, well established before the First World War, was also extended with further laws for coal mines and shops, and minimum wage regulation continued in the 1920s and 1930s – for agricultural workers in 1924 and road haulage ones in 1938. The pattern of government involvement continued in the Second World War, with the same need to insist on arbitration in disputes and prohibit strikes.

Economic and financial change

Taxation

Trends started before the First World War continued in taxation as in industrial relations. Again war quickened them, because the government had to increase taxes to pay for fighting. When prices were rising and discontent was feared, it was unwise to raise the indirect taxes falling on goods and services very greatly. Consequently direct taxes had to increase; 80 per cent of the government's tax income came from them after the First World War, compared with 60 per cent in 1914.

As it seemed right to get more from the wealthy in a national emergency, so there was more progressive taxation. The standard rate of income tax rose from about 6 per cent in 1914 to 30 per cent after the First World War and, although it subsequently fell, it increased again to 50 per cent in the Second World War. Furthermore there were higher death duties and more super-tax levied on the very rich. In the Second World War the highest rate of tax was 19s 6d (about 98p) in £1 received for the top part of very large incomes. While the rich paid a much greater proportion of their incomes in tax, ordinary working-class people also began to pay income tax for the first time in the First World War. The government were careful to ensure that allowances for wives and children made the tax look fairer, and this also meant that workers, being differently affected, were less likely to unite in opposition. Still, the standard rate of income tax came to affect ordinary people and became important in popular politics.

There was also a big rise in taxes on goods. Britain had been a free trade country, where only a few taxes were levied on imports to get money for the government. Now it became a protectionist one where taxes were deliberately used to make foreign items more expensive so as to increase the sale of home manufactures. Other industrial countries, like Germany and the USA, had been protectionist from the late nineteenth century, but up to the First World War Britain had generally prospered from expanding world trade and investment. The long-term problems in basic British industries and resulting structural unemployment in the 1920s were a strong argument for *protection*. The empire could produce food and industrial raw materials while providing a large market for British goods.

Yet when the Conservative leader, Baldwin, suggested protection in 1923 he lost a general election heavily, and when Labour was briefly in power its chancellor of the exchequer, Snowden, deliberately scrapped import taxes. The electorate seemed to think protection meant higher prices rather than more jobs, and until 1932 import duties were only levied for special reasons. A few were introduced in the First World War to serve patriotic needs by getting the little extra money and ensuring people bought British goods. A law in 1921 introduced taxes on a few items like radio valves and particular chemicals which Britain needed to produce at home to be self-sufficient in war. A law in 1925 prevented 'dumping', whereby other countries sold goods in Britain at below cost price to get rid of them.

General taxes between a fifth and a third of the value of manufactured goods were only introduced in 1932 when an economic crisis led to the national government dominated by Conservatives who largely believed in protection and now had the electoral strength to carry it through. They never quite achieved what they wanted – a free trade area throughout the empire where the state would effectively shut out foreign goods and people would buy British or colonial items. Self-governing colonies wanted to protect their own industries with their own taxes. The best British ministers could achieve in negotiations at Ottawa in 1932 was a system of imperial preference whereby lower duties were charged on British and empire goods rather than no taxes at all.

Currency and the economy

There were not only major changes in how the government levied tax in 1914–45 but in how it managed the currency and its whole budget. From 1821 to the First World War Britain had been on the gold standard, which meant that bank notes could be exchanged for gold; £1 was worth a set sum of between a third and a quarter ounce of gold. The value was set; the Bank of England – which was independent of the government – had to ensure it had enough gold reserves to exchange paper money for gold and ministers left the bank to alter its interest rate as necessary to borrow money and keep the appropriate funds.

After the gold standard had to be suspended because of economic disruption from the war, the government could not just leave currency management to the bank. It had hard decisions to make itself. Following the war Britain, like other major industrial countries, decided to return to the gold standard and that the £ should be exchangeable for the same amount of gold as in 1914, which would mean it was worth $4.86 in American currency. This rate of exchange, decided by the government, had vital consequences for British industry and ordinary workers. Economists generally agree that the rate was too high – about 10 per cent too high is the normal calculation – and that made British goods more expensive abroad. If the £ exchanged for $4.86 it followed that an item costing £1 in British money could be bought for $4.86 in the United States. Had the rate been almost 10 per cent lower at, say, $4.40 the item could have traded for only $4.40, and more might have been sold. In other words, a more highly valued £ meant more expensive and fewer exports to the USA and elsewhere, lower industrial production in Britain and greater unemployment – unemployment which was at least partly a direct consequence of a government decision. Workers who found it hard to make goods competitively might reasonably look to the government for some assistance with a problem that it had helped create.

Here came the question of how the government should use its budgets. The traditional view was that the government should levy the taxes to cover its own spending, ensure that it collected as much as it spent, and in this way balance the budget. Some economists and politicians, particularly ones with more left-wing views, stressed how by spending more on employing workers the government might in turn give them more to spend, which would increase demand for goods and services in the country. Generally, though, both

Conservative and Labour governments concentrated on the normal balanced budget.

A different way of thinking was being developed by Keynes. He stressed how if there was high unemployment the government might reasonably borrow in order to spend more. If the government spent the money on, say, building houses or roads, this would not only give jobs to workers directly employed but have a broader effect through what economists call the multiplier. The point is that the money spent by the government will not only be used once but several times. The investment on housing or roads will provide more wages and profits for the workers and capitalists building them, who will spend their income on a variety of goods and services, from fish and chips to Rolls Royces. Not only this, but money used to buy a mass of items like bricks or cement mixers will stimulate further industries and their manufacturers. As this multiplier effect works, so the government can get more taxes from those with larger incomes and balance its budget once again. Hence it follows that in an economic downturn the government should spend more and not worry about its unbalanced budget, which will soon be balanced by extra tax revenues.

In hindsight, Keynes's analysis of the situation in a time of falling prices seems to have much truth in it. While Treasury officials thought that if the government took more by taxing and borrowing there would be less money for ordinary commercial investment, Keynes saw how some wealth was apparently unused. If governments had acted on his ideas they might have revived the economy. Many historians have taken this line since the Second World War, though others have drawn attention to problems. Would the increase in demand necessarily do much to help the industries which were specially depressed and the regions depending on them? What would happen if the money were spent on imports rather than home-produced goods? How great was the multiplier effect and how long would it take to work? The outcome was uncertain, and Keynes was altering his mind on many key issues in the early 1930s. How far can governments be blamed for not following a policy which was not fully worked out or accepted by most economists?

Marked changes came from 1931 when the government abandoned the gold standard because of economic crisis. Interest rates were then lowered, and the Bank of England's rate, which gave signals to other lenders, was 2 per cent. This policy of low interest rates – 'cheap money' as it was called – was intended to encourage industrialists and others to borrow and increase employment.

The American and German governments did invest government money in projects which set people to work, not apparently to follow an economic theory but to meet practical problems. The German government undertook large-scale road building and rearmament, which prepared it for war and revived the economy marvellously. After 1935 the British rearmament programme necessitated by Germany's action also did much for economic revival – whether the government's money went on houses or bombs it still had the stimulating effects Keynes described. In the late 1930s the government did plan an unbalanced budget, but more because of what it had to spend on armaments than because of any economic theory. In the Second World War its approach altered – the government had to manage the nation's economy to fight the war, and Keynes was taken on as a Treasury adviser. In 1941 there was a new type of budget in which the government planned for the overall supply and demand for goods in the economy and calculated the effects of its own taxing and spending plans on these. The state was planning or managing the economy as a whole, not just its own finances. In 1944 a white paper stated the government's 'employment policy', explaining how it would set out to maintain a 'high and stable level of employment' by using government spending and tax rates to boost demand for workers and create more jobs in economic slumps. This may be seen as the triumph of Keynes's ideas, but it also came from a complex mixture of different economic theories, 1930s experience, wartime planning and changing public expectations.

Government and industry

By 1944 the government had experience of controlling individual industries which would have been almost inconceivable in 1914. Before the First World War it sometimes had a role in deciding workers' wages and conditions but rarely prices or management methods. In wartime the state needed controls over trade and production, which not only altered but prevented any free market. During the First World War there were state-run munitions factories, state control of workers and price fixing. Coal mines, railways and much national shipping were taken over by the government to ensure essential war supplies. The state did not nationalise them. Their capitalist owners still got profits, which were supposed to be tightly controlled, and the previous managers generally still ran them on a day-to-day basis, but government ministers could direct and control how they met national needs. Because of shortages of imported food and raw materials, the government eventually bought up over 90 per cent of imports and controlled their prices and distribution. Its control of food supply extended to deciding on land use and, at the end of the war, rationing some basic items as well as fixing their prices. The controls were wide ranging, but they had been introduced in a largely free market economy to meet an emergency, and they went again when the crisis ended. Industries returned to their previous owners and management by the end of 1921, though railways were forced to amalgamate, with further price controls. Regulation for both road and rail carriers meant that they competed for customers on terms decided by the state rather than in a real free market in the 1920s and 1930s.

The government gave subsidies and organised amalgamations both in new industries trying to get going and old industries failing to succeed against competition. It helped achieve the amalgamation of chemical companies which formed Imperial Chemical Industries (ICI) in 1926 and airlines which made up British Overseas Airways in 1939. It provided money for scientific research and imposed import taxes on competing goods to encourage new technologically based industries. Taxes were also put on cotton, iron and steel imports on the understanding that British manufacturers would reorganise and improve efficiency. Coal owners were reluctant to amalgamate but were brought together under the 1930 Coal Mines Act to fix prices and limit output on a local basis. Loans and subsidies were used to encourage shipbuilding when there were few orders in the 1930s. In agriculture there were restrictions on imports and subsidies for farmers from the early 1930s as marketing boards, set up by laws in 1931 and 1933, managed the sale of much produce. All this amounted not to an overall economic plan, but to a rather piecemeal action to keep industries going when they looked in danger. Yet overall it meant a massive change away from the free market.

Before 1945 there was not much nationalisation – state ownership – of firms. Local councils continued to extend their enterprises providing services like water, gas, electricity and tram and bus transport. In 1933 the state created the London Passenger Transport Board, which ran communications in the capital. It also set up the Central Electricity Board which constructed a national grid, but the electricity was actually produced in power stations owned by private companies or local councils. It took a major initiative in establishing the BBC in 1926 with a monopoly of radio broadcasting, so that this developed as a public service paid for by owners' licence fees instead of a commercial affair financed by advertising as in the USA. By 1938 over three-quarters of British homes had radio licences, and the state had significant extra power.

Unemployment

The government did a small amount directly to make jobs for the unemployed. The Unemployment Grants Committee set up in 1928 was soon providing work for about 4 per cent of the jobless. The government would speed up projects like road building when unemployment went up markedly, and tried to tackle the very high local unemployment in areas where basic industries were declining.

First they tried getting the workers to move to the jobs. The Industrial Transference Board helped pay for over a quarter million people to move between 1929 and 1938. The other solution was to get industry to go to the workers. This was done from 1934 by special areas acts to encourage firms to shift to places of very high unemployment in the north and South Wales. At first this was done by supplying extra money for local councils to provide services, but it was extended to include loans and subsidies from the government. It had a small-scale effect; one estimate is that it produced an extra 14,900 jobs by 1938. Still, it marked the beginning of state action to get industry to move according to social needs rather than for market reasons – a 'regional' policy which went much further after the Second World War.

The Second World War

Government control over the economy and society went far further in the Second World War than it had in the First. New ministries were started quickly to run the war effort. Transport was taken over and government directions sent out for farming. Industry generally remained under private ownership, but with government control via instructions about production and a national 'manpower budget' which meant people being allocated to jobs and many women being forced into war work. Thus *collectivism* went much further than ever before. There were more welfare measures, the family means test designed to keep down government spending in the 1930s was scrapped, and many wages boards were set up to raise low-paid workers' income. Corporatism went much further; the minister of labour, Ernest Bevin – himself a major trade union leader – worked with the Joint Consultative Committee of employers and trade unionists.

At the end of the First World War there was a widespread ambition, at least in government, to return to the state of things before the war. After the Second World War there was a widespread desire for change, which was one of the reasons for the election of the first Labour government with a House of Commons majority in 1945. Why had the state's role in the 1920s and 1930s looked unattractive and inadequate to large numbers of people, and should historians accept their judgements and criticisms?

Document case study

The reasons for the 1919 Housing Act

7.1 The minister responsible for the act puts his case to the cabinet

From cabinet memorandum from C. Addison, 11 March 1918

The urgent necessity for a large scheme for building new houses immediately after the war is based on the following considerations:

1 The clearance of slum areas . . .
2 The effects [on] health and physical deterioration of overcrowding and of insanitary and defective housing . . .
3 The effects upon the <u>general standard of life</u> of bad and insufficient housing
4 . . . the effects of bad housing upon <u>Industrial Unrest</u>
5 Food production after the war will be greatly hindered if a large rural housing scheme is not immediately undertaken . . .
6 In the urban districts also . . . it is necessary to have houses for producers to live in.
7 The necessity for providing employment concurrently with <u>rapid demobilisation</u> is one of the strongest arguments . . .
10 Of course the most important reason is that homes must be provided for the returning soldiers and sailors. As Mr Walter Long, when President of the Local Government Board, said:– . . . To let them come from horrible water-logged trenches to something little better than a pigsty here would indeed be criminal on the part of ourselves, and would be a negation of all we have said during this war, that we can never repay those men for what they have done for us.

Source: PRO CAB 24/44 GT3877

7.2 Housing requiring improvement or replacement before the First World War

Slums in the East End of London, December 1912

Source: Hulton Getty Picture Collection

7.3 Inter-war council housing

Wealey Castle housing estate, Birmingham, July 1939

Source: Hulton Getty Picture Collection

7.4 A letter from a trade union official to the cabinet

From the general secretary of the Lanarkshire Miners' County Union, November 1918

I was instructed to write [to] you protesting against the delay in providing houses for the Working Classes, and also to forward our most emphatic protest against rents that are being charged for the houses which have already been built by the County Council . . . In any case there is no doubt that the rents which are being proposed for houses that are to be built are out of all proportion to the ability of the working class in this District to pay.

Source: L. F. Orbach, *Homes for heroes: a study of the evolution of British public housing, 1915–1921*, London, 1977, p. 67

7.5 The prime minister's public view

Lloyd George to a meeting of Liberal supporters in Downing Street

The Prime Minister spoke of the need of a great housing programme, and the bringing of light and beauty into the lives of the people. He said:– We must have habitations fit for the heroes who have won the war . . .

Source: *The Times*, 13 November 1918

Lloyd George to a public meeting at Wolverhampton

A vigorous community, strong, healthy men and women, is more valuable even from the commercial and industrial point of view than a community which is below par in consequence of bad conditions. Treat it, if you like, not as a human proposition, but as a business proposition. It is good business to see that the men, the women and the children are brought up and sustained under conditions that will give strength and vigour to their frames, more penetration and endurance to their intelligence, and more spirit and heart than ever to face the problems of life, which will always be problems that will require fighting right from the cradle to the tomb. That is the first problem. One of the ways of dealing with that is, of course, to deal with the housing conditions. Slums are not fit homes for the men who have won this war or for their children. They are not fit nurseries for the children who are to make an Imperial race, and there must be no patching up. This problem has got to be undertaken in a way never undertaken before, as a great national charge and duty . . .

Source: *The Times*, 25 November 1918

7.6 The prime minister speaks to the cabinet

In a short time we might have three-quarters of Europe converted to Bolshevism . . . He believed that Great Britain would hold out, but only if the people were given a sense of confidence . . . We had promised them reforms time and again, but little had been done. We must give them the conviction this time that we meant it, and we must give them that conviction quickly . . .

Even if it cost a hundred million pounds, what was that compared to the stability of the State?

So long as we could persuade the people that we were prepared to help them and to meet them in their aspirations, he believed that the sane and steady leaders among the workers would have an easy victory over the Bolsheviks among them.

Source: PRO CAB 23/9 WC539, 3 March 1919, quoted in M. Swenarton, *Homes fit for heroes: the politics and architecture of early state housing in Britain*, London, 1981, p. 78

Document case-study questions

1 Compare Documents 7.1 and 7.5. Which of the points listed in Document 7.1 does Lloyd George also mention or develop in the extracts in Document 7.5?

2 In what ways do Documents 7.1, 7.4 and 7.6 suggest that fear of revolution was a reason for the government bringing in the 1919 Housing Act?

3 What are the obvious differences between the housing shown in the photographs in 7.2 and 7.3? How would the Wealey Castle estate have been a healthier neighbourhood than the slums?

4 In Document 7.1, Addison indicates that the duty to provide new housing for returning troops is the most important reason for reform. From these documents and your own knowledge and understanding explain why some recent historians have emphasised the fear of revolution as the most important reason.

Notes and references

1 R. M. Titmuss, *Problems of social policy*, London, 1950. For a summary of debate on the effects of war see the introduction in A. Marwick, *The deluge*, 2nd edn, London, 1991.

Conclusion:
problematic progress and doubtful definitions

What historians write depends on when they are writing, and this conclusion is written from a viewpoint in 1997. Ideas about democracy and the role of the state have altered and varied through the twentieth century, and the changes are reflected in the sort of history books produced. Much of the writing is influenced by the idea of progress – that there is some kind of sustained change in one particular direction and that it involves improvement. Moves towards greater democracy and an expanding role for the state are often seen as progress. Those who favoured or advanced them are described in phrases which suggest they were progressive and perceptive; those who opposed them are often viewed as backward looking or failing to understand current problems.

Democracy and representation

There are many different definitions of democracy. The broadest is 'government by the people'. This is generally seen as good or progressive, but there are many different views about the type and extent of democracy we should have.

There are features of Britain's democracy which are distinctive or controversial. Britain's executive (what we normally call the government, headed by a prime minister) is chosen from its legislature (the parliament which has to approve laws and taxes). Using the system of party whips, the British executive has a great deal of control over legislation (see Chapter 4). Most electors, therefore, vote to choose party leaders who will form the government, rather than thinking about the individual MPs who make up the House of Commons. This contrasts, for example, with the USA where there is one election to choose a president, who heads the executive, and separate ones for the Congress, which has most law-making power. Does a British elector's single vote give adequate choice?

Britain has what we call a representative democracy. Electors choose MPs as their representatives. Although it is widely assumed that they are chosen to carry out all the policies in their party's manifesto, there is a long-standing belief that they are elected to use their personal judgement on issues. Voters have chosen them as representatives because they trust them to make the right decisions, rather than as delegates with instructions on how to vote.

Although MPs are meant to represent roughly equal numbers of people, there has been deliberate over-representation of Ireland, Scotland and Wales. Ireland was allocated 101 MPs in 1801 and, despite a falling population, kept them to the end of the First World War when, according to the number of electors, it should have had 63. When separate boundary commissions were established for the three countries in 1944, Scotland and Wales were allocated more MPs in relation to population than England was.

The British House of Commons is representative in the sense that it is chosen by its people. It is not representative in the sense of being typical of the population as a whole. Women and ethnic minorities have been under-represented in the twentieth century. It is certainly not representative of people by social class, large numbers of professional *middle-class* MPs – like lawyers and teachers – contrasting with small numbers of manual workers. Should parliament be representative in being typical of the population as well as chosen by it?

Different systems of voting – is Britain a democracy?

Many would say that in a democracy the government is chosen by a majority of the people and that each person's vote counts equally. It is easy to argue that this is not true in twentieth-century Britain. No twentieth-century government elected since 1935 has received over 50 per cent of the votes for its party's candidates. Only about half the parliamentary votes cast in Britain in recent years have been 'effective votes' which helped elect an MP; 51.8 per cent were in the 1997 election. Those cast for unsuccessful candidates have not helped to give the voter any say in the House of Commons.

PR systems could ensure that votes count more equally and AV systems could prevent candidates being elected to parliament by a minority of voters (see p. 43). The first-past-the-post system, which is simple and helps produce strong governments, has become general in the English-speaking world – not only in the UK but in North America and India. This contrasts with Europe, where PR is more usual, and might seem to reflect some basic cultural differences. Looking at the story here, Britain's system seems to have developed in uncertain and accidental ways. Two-member *constituencies* were usual in Britain until 1885. The arrangement introduced for large towns in 1867, with each elector having two votes to select three MPs, was designed to ensure some representation for minorities – one of the key principles of PR. The general system of single-member constituencies was introduced in 1885 and developed as a compromise from negotiations between party leaders. Some people with degrees could also elect MPs to represent universities, and several of these elections were carried out by PR until the abolition of university representation in 1948.

Most western European countries opted for a PR system after the First World War; all except the UK had one by 1920. Britain nearly did the same. Following the Speaker's Conference recommendation for electoral reform, the House of Commons favoured AV and the House of Lords PR (see pp. 43–44). The Commons itself rejected PR by only eight votes on one occasion. Out of the disagreements came a compromise or deadlock which meant that first-past-the-post continued and came to seem part of the twentieth-century British way of life. In 1931 there was nearly change again when a Labour government depending on Liberal support introduced a bill for AV which was stopped by the House of Lords (see p. 46). Had the government survived two years longer, it would presumably have made the change when the House of Lords could no longer delay it under the terms of the 1911 Parliament Act.

While Britain came very near to electoral reform, there was one major reason why it did not happen. PR, in particular, was always a cause for minorities. Some Conservatives favoured it in the late nineteenth century when they feared being overwhelmed by a *working-class* electorate; Irish unionists suggested it for a new Irish parliament when they saw themselves outnumbered there; Labour as a fringe party advocated it before 1914; the Liberals as a minority wanted it from the 1920s; but any party which actually got power would oppose it – at least until 1997.

Media

Voters must be able to learn about a variety of political parties and beliefs if they are to have real choice in a democracy. A range of newspapers and broadcasting companies serve the British elector, but there may still be problems. Governments can control broadcasting by various laws and by appointing members of the BBC and the Independent Television Commission (ITC). The press has capitalist owners, who appear to have massive influence on British public opinion.

Progress towards democracy

Overall the increase in voters and information available makes Britain far more democratic in 1945 and 1997 than in 1830, but progress has not been as clear or continuous as people often assume. The 1832 Reform Act, for example, may have reduced the working-class electorate and specifically stopped women voting. Partly as a result, nineteenth-century parliamentary politics developed as an exclusively male affair. Many of the arguments against female suffrage around 1900 appear absurd a century later.

In some ways there was more participation in politics and possibly a better-informed electorate in the nineteenth century than in the late twentieth. The large processions and street demonstrations of the early nineteenth century show that more people took part publicly in politics. The rapid growth and enthusiasm for local political clubs in the later nineteenth century contrasts with a long-term decline in political party membership in the second half of the twentieth century. Victorian national newspapers, which admittedly had a comparatively small circulation, carried lengthy reports of parliamentary proceedings and the full text of speeches by top politicians. Complex arguments were therefore available to the public, whereas the late twentieth century has seen a decline in parliamentary reporting and a growing emphasis on 'sound bites' – phrases giving simplified messages which are likely to be repeated on television news bulletins. The range of broadcast coverage, including the televising of parliament, gives more political news, but there are questions about the type of coverage and participation as well as about the amount.

Some problems with the democratic process have remained remarkably similar. The quality of coverage in popular newspapers has worried people ever since their development a century ago. Lord Salisbury disparaged the *Daily Mail* as a paper 'written by office boys for office boys'. Politicians who depend on party political activists have to take account of their views, which are often extreme and very different from those of the electorate as a whole. It was a dilemma in the late nineteenth-century Liberal party (see pp. 27–28) and caused a crisis for Labour in the 1980s, so that their leaders spent a decade breaking down the influence of left-wing constituency workers. In the nineteenth century there was a long campaign against *patronage* – by which men in power promoted those they knew to well-paid government jobs. Similar concern arose over Conservative appointments to quangos (quasi-autonomous non-governmental organisations) in the 1980s and 1990s, though the patronage was on a far smaller scale.

The role of the state: collectivism, corporatism and individual freedom

Between 1830 and 1945 there was a long-term move towards *collectivism* – the belief that the government should act for the community as a whole and that the welfare of individuals was the concern of the state. Between 1905 and 1945 a number of reforms were made which helped towards the full creation of a welfare state in 1945–50. Having a welfare state meant the government guaranteed all citizens a basic minimum income and the services needed for a fulfilling life, particularly health care, housing and education. It went together with a need to keep unemployment down and a state acceptance of equal rights and community responsibilities.

This was accompanied by a state commitment to regulate the economy as a whole and take over or supervise essential services like transport and energy. The commitment was becoming clear by 1945, and there was large-scale nationalisation and extensive economic planning afterwards. Corporatism, where the government worked together with powerful economic groups, seemed another essential part of the process and involved a particularly important role for trade unions.

All these trends continued with quite broad acceptance to the 1970s, and historians generally wrote about them as types of progress. Many are still generally accepted in the 1990s. All the main political parties have consistently pledged to maintain or increase spending on the National Health Service. Conservative and Labour government schemes for tackling unemployment show that both main parties accept a state responsibility to deal with it. It is taken for granted that government budgets must be planned to regulate demand in the economy as a whole and not just to manage the state's own finances. Recent governments have consistently used 'regional policies' to encourage industrialists to develop businesses in areas with high unemployment. From a viewpoint in 1997, therefore, it might be reasonable to see the development of such policies since 1945 as progress.

Some of the trends recorded in this book have, however, been reversed. Increasing state and local control of public services, which led to large-scale nationalisation after the Second World War, has generally been abandoned. There is a widespread view that private enterprise works better than state or municipal management. The growth in state planning and corporatist arrangements which increased trade union power was widely discredited by failures in the 1970s, although the European Union is more favourable to these ideas than British governments in the 1990s.

Historians and economists have increasingly questioned the assumptions which underlie collectivism and state planning. Above all, has the state spent too much money when it would have been better for economic growth and personal freedom to leave it with individuals? Correlli Barnett[1] suggested that from the Second World War too much was spent on social welfare rather than industrial investment. Was the state making too many decisions which should have been left to ordinary consumers? Did the ideas of positive freedom (see pp. 75–76) and collectivism give the government too much power? Whereas writing on the twentieth-century economy from 1945 to the 1970s was frequently dominated by Keynes's ideas, commentators in the 1980s and 1990s have often been more influenced by Friedrich Hayek, who emphasised the dangers of state power in *The road to serfdom*, published near the end of the Second World War.

Although twentieth-century discussion about the state is often dominated by economic questions, its most basic function is protecting individuals against outside danger – maintaining defence and order. This justification of the state's role has been the basis of much political theory so that conscription – forcing men to fight in the army and possibly die for their country – raises crucial problems. Lord Salisbury, speaking of it as prime minister in 1900, said, 'no-one imagines even among the youngest of us, that he will ever live to see conscription adopted in this country'. It was adopted 16 years later in the First World War, and this emphasises both how much events change the state's role and how problematic the idea of progress is.

Notes and references

1 C. Barnett, *The audit of war, the illusion and reality of Britain as a great nation*, London, 1986.

Select bibliography

Useful and perceptive books on changes towards democracy and the role of the state are:
B. Harrison, *The transformation of British politics 1860–1995*, Oxford, 1996; M. Pugh, *The making of modern British politics, 1867–1939*, 2nd edn, Oxford, 1993; M. Pugh, *State and society*, London, 1994; and D. Read, *The age of urban democracy*, London, 1994.

Parliamentary reform and the development of party politics

For the First Reform Act, see M. Brock, *The Great Reform Act*, London, 1973. For the Second Reform Act, see F. B. Smith, *The making of the Second Reform Bill*, Cambridge, 1966. For the Third Reform Act, see A. Jones, *The politics of reform 1884*, Cambridge, 1972.

Shorter books or pamphlets giving a useful summary are: J. Belchem, *Class, party and the political system in Britain 1867–1914*, Historical Association, 1990; E. J. Evans, *The Great Reform Act*, 2nd edn, London, 1994; M. Pugh, *The evolution of the British electoral system 1832–1987*, Historical Association, 1988; and J. K. Walton, *The Second Reform Act*, London, 1987.

For the electoral system after the First Reform Act, N. Gash, *Politics in the age of Peel*, 2nd edn, London, 1977, is a classic work, as is H. J. Hanham, *Elections and party management: politics in the time of Disraeli and Gladstone*, 2nd edn, London, 1978, for the later period.

For the development of the Conservative party, see R. Blake, *The Conservative party from Peel to Thatcher*, 2nd edn, London, 1997; B. Coleman, *Conservatism and the Conservative party in nineteenth-century Britain*, London, 1988; R. Stewart, *The foundation of the Conservative party 1830–1867*, London, 1978; R. Shannon, *The age of Disraeli 1868–1881: the rise of Tory democracy*, London, 1992; R. Shannon, *The age of Salisbury 1881–1902: unionism and empire*, London, 1996; S. Ball, *The Conservative party and British politics 1902–1951*, London, 1995; and J. A. Ramsden, *The age of Balfour and Baldwin 1902–40*, London, 1978.

For the Liberal party, see T. A. Jenkins, *The Liberal ascendancy 1830–1886*, London, 1994; J. Vincent, *The formation of the British Liberal party 1857–68*, 2nd edn, Brighton, 1976; J. R. Parry, *The rise and fall of Liberal government in Victorian Britain*, Yale, 1993; and G. R. Searle, *The Liberal party, triumph and disintegration 1886–1929*, London, 1992.

For women's suffrage and electoral changes in the First World War, see M. Pugh, *Votes for women in Britain 1867–1928*, Historical Association, 1994; M. Pugh, *Electoral reform in war and peace 1906–1918*, London, 1978; and M. Pugh, *Women and the women's movement in Britain, 1914–1959*, London, 1992. For the suffragettes, see A. Rosen, *Rise up women! The militant campaign of the Women's Social and Political Union 1903–1914*, London, 1974.

Useful articles about parliamentary reform include: E. F. Biagini, 'Liberalism and the new electorate after 1867', *History Review*, no. 10 (1996); M. Cole and D. Hartley, '1832: an unseen advance for democracy?', *Modern History Review (MHR)*, vol. 9, no. 2 (1997); J. Derry, 'Earl Grey and reform', *MHR*, vol. 6, no. 4 (1995); J. Garrard, 'Educating the masters: urban political parties and the new voters after 1867', *History Sixth*, no. 9 (1991); B. Harrison, 'The First World War and feminism in Britain', *History Review*, no. 16 (1993); S. Newman, 'Votes for women', *History Review*, no. 24 (1996); M. Pugh and B. Harrison, 'Perspectives: women's suffrage', *MHR*, vol. 2, no. 1 (1990); M. Pugh, 'Parliamentary reforms in the 1880s: cause and consequence',

MHR, vol. 4, no. 1 (1992); M. Pugh, 'Why did it take so long to achieve votes for women?', *MHR*, vol. 8, no. 4 (1997); M. Pugh, 'Suffragettes caught the camera's eye but hid the extent of the women's movement', *New Perspective*, vol. 3, no. 1 (1997); E. A. Smith, 'Grey and the 1832 Reform Act: how liberal was Grey?', *New Perspective*, vol. 1, no. 1 (1995); P. Smith, '"Leap in the dark": the 1867 Reform Act', *MHR*, vol. 2, no. 1 (1990); and R. Stewart, 'Party in the age of Peel and Palmerston', *History Review*, no. 21 (1995).

Other articles about reform worth attention are: J. P. D. Dunbabin, 'Electoral reforms and their outcome in the United Kingdom 1865–1900' and J. Garrard, 'Parties, members and voters after 1867', in T. R. Gourvish and A. O'Day (eds.), *Later Victorian Britain 1867–1900*, London, 1988; K. T. Hoppen, 'The franchise and electoral politics in England and Ireland 1832–1885', *History*, vol. 70 (1985); and K. T. Hoppen, 'Roads to democracy: electioneering and corruption in nineteenth-century England and Ireland', *History*, vol. 81 (1996).

Power in the state

For a summary of Victorian political development, see T. A. Jenkins, *Parliament, party and politics in Victorian Britain*, Manchester, 1996. For the distribution of power in the state, see G. H. L. May, *The Victorian constitution, conventions and contingencies*, London, 1979. For the cabinet, see G. W. Cox, *The efficient secret, the cabinet and the development of political parties in Victorian England*, Cambridge, 1987. For the role of the monarchy, see F. M. Hardie, *The political influence of the British monarchy, 1868–1952*, London, 1970. For the House of Lords and aristocratic influence, see D. Cannadine, *The decline and fall of the British aristocracy*, Yale, 1990; and E. A. Smith, *The House of Lords in British politics and society 1815–1911*, London, 1992.

For the changing power structure and the role of state, see V. Cromwell, *Revolution or evolution, British government in the nineteenth century*, London, 1977; and J. E. Cronin, *The politics of state expansion: war, state and society in twentieth-century Britain*, London, 1991.

The role of the state

Detailed and useful textbook summaries can be found in: S. G. Checkland, *British public policy 1776–1939, an economic, social and political perspective*, Cambridge, 1983; G. C. Peden, *British economic and social policy: Lloyd George to Margaret Thatcher*, Oxford, 1985; and J. Harris, 'Society and the state in twentieth-century Britain', in F. M. L. Thompson (ed.), *Cambridge social history of Britain 1750–1950*, vol. 3.

For welfare reform, an excellent textbook is D. Fraser, *The evolution of the British welfare state*, 2nd edn, London, 1984. Also see A. Crowther, *British social policy 1914–1939*, London, 1988; and P. Thane, *Foundations of the welfare state*, London, 1982. For a recent interpretation of the 1834 poor law see P. Mandler, 'The new poor law', *MHR*, vol. 5, no. 2 (1993). On Liberal welfare reforms, see M. Pugh, 'Lloyd George, the working class and social reform', *History Review*, no. 10 (1991).

Important biographies of men with a key role in the welfare state include: J. Grigg, *Lloyd George, the people's champion, 1902–1911*, London, 1991; J. Grigg, *Lloyd George, from peace to war, 1912–1916*, London, 1985; and J. Harris, *William Beveridge, a biography*, 2nd edn, Oxford, 1997. M. Pugh, *Lloyd George*, London, 1988, gives a short summary of issues in Lloyd George's career.

Glossary

Anglican	refers to the Church of England and churches connected to it with the same type of worship and organisation
apprenticeship laws	laws which required people to work under someone else's supervision, normally learning skills, for several years before they could earn full wages or undertake certain occupations on their own
aristocracy	those in families with titles or conspicuous wealth who generally own large landed estates
borough	a town (or occasionally a smaller settlement) which has a corporation (council) and rights to run its own affairs originally granted by royal charter
civil servants	people employed by the government in a civil job (outside the police or armed forces)
collectivism	beliefs that the state should have more control over the life and wealth of the country so that it can do more for the community as a whole
constituencies	areas into which the country is divided to elect MPs
free market economy	an economy where people buy and exchange goods freely among themselves, and employers and workers bargain over pay and working conditions without government regulation
Justices of the Peace (JPs)	magistrates who act as judges in courts dealing with minor offences against the law. Until 1888 they had extensive responsibilities to run local government outside boroughs. They were unpaid and generally chosen from among wealthy local employers.
magistrates	*see* Justices of the Peace
middle class	normally people in professions (doing skilled mental work) or owning businesses from which they gain a profit; a general term for those between the large-scale landowners and the working class
Nonconformist	refers to those who had churches separate from the Church of England, originally established because they did not conform with Anglican ideas. They generally had a plainer, more extreme Protestant form of worship and included Methodists, Baptists and many other groups.

opinion polls	questions put to a sample of people (normally 1–3,000) who are chosen to make up a representative cross-section of a larger group
patronage	the power which some ministers and officials have to provide jobs and different benefits for other people
pauper	a person receiving poor relief (money or other benefits provided from local taxes called 'poor rates')
protection	a policy of encouraging people to buy home-produced goods rather than foreign ones by taxing or restricting imports
radicalism	beliefs that how a country is governed should be extensively changed
socialism	beliefs that people should be more equal in wealth. This may be achieved by the state taking over the means of producing wealth or using money from taxation to help the community and especially poorer people in it.
structural unemployment	unemployment due to long-term economic changes which bring about a decline in some industries nationally or regionally
suffragettes	supporters of the Women's Social and Political Union who often used illegal and violent methods to get the vote for women
suffragists	those who campaigned in non-violent and legal ways to get the vote for women
working class	generally understood as people (together with their families) who work with their hands or work for others as wage labourers

Public health and housing	Poverty and individual welfare	
		1830
	1834 **Poor Law Amendment Act** restricts poor relief	1834
		1838
		1842
		1846
		1850
		1854
		1858
		1862
		1866
		1870
1872 **Public Health Act** creates sanitary authorities with medical officers		1874
1875 **Artisans' Dwelling Act** encourages slum clearance		1878
		1882
1885 and 1890 **Housing of the working classes acts** allow council house building		1886
		1890
		1894
		1898
		1902
	1906 **Education Act** allows local councils to provide free school meals	1906
	1908 **Old-age pensions**	1910
	1911 **National Insurance Act** introduces health and unemployment insurance	1914
1919 **Housing Act** starts large-scale council house building	1920 **Unemployment insurance** extended to most workers	1918
		1922
		1926
		1930
		1934
		1938
	1942 **Beveridge report** on social insurance and allied services	1942
	1945 **Family allowances**	

Index